Butterflies
of the Lower
Rio Grande Valley

Butterflies of the Lower Rio Grande Valley

Roland H. Wauer

Johnson Books
BOULDER

Spring Creek Press
ESTES PARK

Published by Johnson Books, a division of Johnson Publishing Company, 1880 South 57th Court, Boulder, Colorado 80301. E-mail: books@jpcolorado.com www.johnsonbooks.com

Composition and design by Eric Christensen
Cover photos by the author

9 8 7 6 5 4 3 2 1

Library of Congress Cataloging-in-Publication Data
Wauer, Roland H.
    Butterflies of the Lower Rio Grande Valley / Roland H. Wauer
        p. cm.
    ISBN 1-55566-347-8
    1. Butterflies—Texas—Lower Rio Grande Valley. I. Title.
    QL551.T4W37 2004
    595.7'89'097644—dc22   2004010441

Printed in the United States by
Johnson Printing
1880 South 57th Court
Boulder, Colorado 80301

Contents

Preface

No place in North America deserves its own regional butterfly guide more than the Lower Rio Grande Valley (LRGV) of Texas. No other area of North America offers so many species—many of which occur nowhere else north of the border—and attracts so many butterfly enthusiasts. A guide to the LRGV butterflies is long overdue.

As my principal interest turned from birds to butterflies over the last several years, numerous friends encouraged me to undertake such a project. Although I have been in complete agreement about the importance of such a guide, other projects and the need to include as many of my own photographs as possible in such a guide have held me back. But when Scott Roederer of Spring Creek Press, an imprint of Johnson Books, contacted me about undertaking such a project, and I discovered that the publisher was willing to commit the necessary resources, I decided now was the time.

For the last several years, I have photographed butterflies in the Valley, throughout most of Texas, and also in adjacent Mexico, all with such a project in mind. I have accumulated several thousand slides, covering the majority of the species that have been recorded in the LRGV. But I have not been so fortunate as to be in the right places at the right times to photograph all of the more unusual strays. Therefore, friends who were more fortunate than I provided several of the photos within; each is credited in the Acknowledgments.

The intent of this field guide is to help the user find and identify the various butterfly species of the LRGV, as well as to obtain a better understanding of their requirements. This book is not intended to discuss butterfly biology or butterfly collecting. Several other publications, many of which are included in Appendix 3, References, provide information on the myriad of interesting subjects relating to butterflies.

Acknowledgments

I have been a butterfly enthusiast for less than a dozen years, but I was fortunate during those years to have been associated with several individuals far more knowledgeable than I. I want to thank those individuals who provided me with an initial introduction to butterflies, both in the field and otherwise. Alphabetically, they include Chris Durden, Paul Miliotis, Mike Overton, Mike Quinn, and John Tveten.

I also want to thank a few additional individuals who have given me support from the very start of this project. Ben Basham and Dave Hanson, both winter residents of the LRGV, have gone out of their way to help in every way possible. Ben provided current information and helped locate necessary photographs of the butterflies. Dave put all of his excellent images at my disposal. Many come from his CD collection of photos, *Butterflies of South Texas*, available at retail outlets in the LRGV. Additional support was provided by Bob Behrstock, Bill Bouton, David and Jan Dauphin, Wanda Demeron, Kim Garwood, Jerry McWilliams, Derek Muschalek, and Mike Quinn.

The majority of the photographs of the butterflies in this book were taken by the author. The following individuals provided additional photographs:

Ben Basham: Polydamas Swallowtail, Dark Kite-Swallowtail, Yellow Angled-Sulphur (b), Gold-bordered Hairstreak, Marius Hairstreak, Tropical Greenstreak, Blue-eyed Sailor (b), Red Cracker (b), Pale-spotted Leafwing (b), White-crescent Longtail, and Frosted Flasher.

Bob Behrstock: Black Crescent, Jalapus Cloudywing, and Small-spotted Skipperling.

Evi Buckner-Opler: Pronus Longtail.

Priscilla and Hank Brodkin: Orion Cecropian, Emerald Aguna, and Stallings' Flat.

Will Carter: Three-tailed Swallowtail, Klug's Clearwing, Mottled Longtail, White-tailed Longtail, and Red-studded Skipper.

Elizabeth Cavazos: Costa-spotted Mimic-White.

Herb Clarke: West Coast Lady, Saltbush Sootywing (b), and Tropical Least Skipper.

Kim Garwood: Muted Hairstreak and Small-spotted Flasher.

Dave Hanson: Broad-banded Swallowtail, Giant White (a, b), Orange-barred Sulphur (b), Silver-banded Hairstreak (b), Xami Hairstreak (b), Ruddy Hairstreak, Mountain Groundstreak, Rawson's Metalmark, Banded Orange Heliconian, Pearl Crescent (b), Tropical Buckeye (b), Band-celled Sister, Guatemalan Cracker (b), Empress Leilia (b), Beautiful Beamer, Teleus Longtail (a, b), Two-barred Flasher, Starred Skipper, Desert Checkered-Skipper (b), Double-dotted Skipper (a, b), Southern Skipperwing, Common Mellana (a, b), Olive-clouded Skipper, Hecebolus Skipper (a, b), and Yucca Giant-Skipper.

Frank Hedges: Banded Patch.

Greg Lasley: Texan Crescent (b).

Paul Opler: Telea Hairstreak and Double-striped Longtail.

Jeff Pippen: Dina Yellow

Jerry McWilliams: Yellow Angled-Sulphur (a), Goodson's Green-streak, Red-lined Scrub-Hairstreak, Cyna Blue, Rosita Patch, Common Banner, Pale-spotted Leafwing (a), and Hammock Skipper.

Mike Quinn: Red-spotted Patch and Broken Silverdrop.

Ellie Thompson: Tailed Sulphur, Mercurial Skipper, Fritzgaertner's Flat, and Evans' Skipper.

During the last several years, a number of individuals kindly examined slides of butterflies to identify and/or verify their subjects. Those individuals include Charles Bordelon, Nick Grishin, Ed Knudson, Paul Opler, Mike Overton, Mike Quinn, and Andy Warren. I thank them one and all.

There also is a much larger set of folks who have provided me with species lists for various sites in the LRGV. Those lists, along with numerous reports and publications (many of which are included in the References section), form the baseline for what is currently known about when and where the butterflies occur in the LRGV. This group includes (with some redundancy) Ben Basham, Bob Behrstock, Carrie Cate, Buck and Linda Cooper, David and Jan Dauphin, Terry Fuller, Jeff Glassberg, Mike Hannisian, Dave Hanson, David and Ednelza Henderson, P.D. Hulce, Ed Knudson, Richard Lehman, Jerry McWilliams, Derek Muschalek, Floyd and June Preston, Charlie Sassine, Ellie Thompson, and John Tveten.

Finally, three additional individuals provided significant support for this project in other ways that are essential to the success of such a venture. Mark Elwonger kindly provided the map of the LRGV. Scott Roederer provided considerable encouragement and major assistance with the manuscript. Because of his competent and careful review of the manuscript, inconsistencies, errors, and redundancies have been held to a minimum. Any errors that still might exist are the fault of the author. And third, but certainly not last, my wife, Betty, was a constant support throughout the process. She helped scan slides and came to my aid on computer questions on numerous occasions. I am most appreciative to them all!

How to Use This Guide

This guide is for everyone, even those who are only thinking about watching butterflies in the Lower Rio Grande Valley (LRGV). Although it will be most beneficial to beginners, even experts will appreciate the wide assortment of images of live butterflies. Photographs of some of these butterflies are not available in any other field guide.

Such an array of species provides a rather unusual opportunity for visual comparisons. The descriptive narratives offer insight into each of the LRGV species, providing a comprehensive source of information not previously available within any single reference.

The introductory section that follows provides important information on how to use this book to its fullest advantage.

Butterfly Identification

The hobby of butterfly watching—locating, studying, and identifying them—has grown exponentially in recent years. The interest in butterflies has expanded from a few professional lepidopterists intent on studying a species or a population to an ever-increasing number of amateur enthusiasts who watch butterflies for the simple pleasure of spending time outdoors with a charismatic and fascinating group of wildlife. Although many folks are content with simply watching butterflies and perhaps attracting them to a garden, the majority of people sooner or later want to identify all those they observe. If you are one of those people, this book is especially for you.

Butterfly identification is the next step beyond simply watching them, but it requires at least two tools: a field guide and close-focusing binoculars. This book is a regional field guide. Several of the more comprehensive field guides—those that cover either the western or eastern half of North America or all of North America—are listed in Appendix 2, References.

Binoculars are essential, and close-focusing binoculars, those that focus to six feet or less, are necessary for identifying many butterflies, especially the smaller ones and those with intricate patterns that require careful study. Binoculars that lack close-focusing capability require the observer to stand so far away that the butterfly's features and shape can seldom be seen well enough.

Locating most species of butterflies takes very little practice. It is simply a matter of walking through a garden or along a roadway or trail and spotting one. But identifying your subject is not as easy. Here are a few tips for beginners.

First, stop several feet away, not allowing your shadow to fall across the butterfly; a sudden shadow will often frighten it away. From that position, examine your subject through your binoculars, noting its size, shape, color, and pattern. These features are all important, but you may face difficulties with each of them.

Size alone is not enough, of course. For one thing, individuals of the same butterfly species can vary in size as much as forty percent, depending upon the nutrients that were available to them as caterpillars. Shape can be extremely important, but worn individuals or those with missing pieces of the wing or tail (either from wear or damage by a predator) must be considered closely. Color is important, but keep in mind that colors start fading after a few days.

Wing patterns—spots, bars, and bands and where they occur—are usually most important in identifying your subject. Here again, worn individuals can lose scales that provide an essential clue.

All four of these features may be required for correct identification. Even if you observe all the features, a small number of species cannot be identified in the field; a careful examination of the genitalia is sometimes necessary. That close-up encounter is best left to the lepidopterist.

Butterfly Features and Terms
Specific terms for describing butterfly features are used throughout the book. Although many are self-explanatory, such as upperside and

underside, others are terms used by lepidopterists when describing butterfly features, and they require some definition. A glossary is included in Appendix 1 to help with those more scientific terms. Figure 1 (*page 4*) shows the terms used for describing the key features of butterflies when identifying species in the field.

Studying Your Field Guide

It is important to study your field guide before using it in the field, especially to become familiar with where the species are located in the book. Like birds, butterflies are grouped in families and subfamilies. An initial understanding of these groups, where a butterfly may fit into them, and where to find those groups in your field guide will speed up your identifications greatly.

For example, swallowtails are large, are usually yellow and/or black, and often have a noticeable tail. Sulphurs can be small to large in size, but they are almost always yellow with black markings. Metalmarks, on the other hand, are small and typically have metallic streaks or other markings. Leafwings are medium to large with cryptic underwings but orange-red upperwings. Grass-skippers are medium to small and usually rest with folded wings; their flight is often rapid and skipping, hence their name. The section on each family and subfamily included in this book begins with a brief description of their characteristics.

Butterfly identification requires patience and practice, but by carefully studying your subject and matching its features to the photographs in this field guide, you'll make the correct determination.

The Format of This Book

This book has an introductory chapter, "The Lower Rio Grande Valley," which sets the stage and provides an introduction to the biogeography of the Valley. This chapter also includes a brief description of the twenty best LRGV sites for finding butterflies.

The section following that chapter—"Butterflies of the Lower Rio Grande Valley"—is the heart of this book. It is divided into the six

Antennae

Club

Palps

Leading Edge

Basal Area

Bars

Forewing

Outer
Angle

Eyespots

Hindwing

Trailing Edge

Fringe

Marginal
Band

Submarginal
Band

Upperside

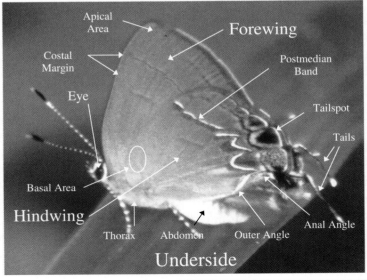

Apical
Area

Forewing

Costal
Margin

Postmedian
Band

Eye

Tailspot

Tails

Basal Area

Hindwing

Thorax

Abdomen

Outer Angle

Anal Angle

Underside

families of butterflies, and the families are further divided into pertinent subfamilies. Each division begins with a brief description of the family or subfamily. Following that is an account of each of the LRGV species, divided into four categories: Description, When and Where, Similar Species, and Remarks.

"Description" includes the butterfly's general physical details, key features, and its wingspan in inches. The information in this part of the account is designed to enhance species identification. The specialty species—those that do not normally occur elsewhere in the United States—are highlighted by the term "**LRGV specialty**" in boldface to draw attention to their relative importance.

Each description reflects the typical position in which the butterfly is likely to be seen. The narrative begins with upperside descriptions for those species that usually perch with open wings, such as swallowtails and spread-wing skippers. It begins with underside descriptions for those species that typically perch with closed wings, such as sulphurs and grass-skippers.

"When and Where" begins with a general statement on the relative abundance of the species, using specific status terms. An explanation of those terms appears in the introduction to the species accounts and in the checklist in Appendix 3. The months the species has been recorded follow the status, if known.

Suggestions for where the butterfly may be seen are given next. For instance, some species frequent open fields, while others are most likely to be found in shaded woodlands. Some species prefer the coastal areas, while others are more likely to occur in the drier western portion of the LRGV. And because butterflies are so closely tied to their larval foodplants, pertinent plant species are mentioned as well.

"Similar Species" covers the species that could most likely be confused with the butterfly and gives key features to help differentiate them. This section is most valuable to the novice who is trying to decide between two or more similar species. Examples include such look-alike

species as Giant and Ornython swallowtails, Little and Mimosa yellows, and Clench's, Goodson's, and Tropical greenstreaks.

"Remarks" includes a wide variety of additional information that does not fit elsewhere. It may include helpful or interesting quotes, relationships, natural history, or the butterfly's other common and/or scientific names.

Butterfly Photographs

Most species are shown using a single image of the most common view, upperside or underside. The other view may also be included when it is very different or when it differs because of sexual or seasonal dimorphism.

Most of the images are personal photographs (slides) I've taken over the last several years. About half of those were taken within the LRGV, while the majority of the others were taken in northeastern Mexico. Many of the LRGV specialties are far more numerous and, therefore, more readily photographed in nearby Mexico. I made several trips into the adjacent Mexican states of Tamaulipas and San Luis Potosi between 1998 and January 2004. A few photographs were also taken elsewhere in Texas. Additional pictures were obtained from friends and colleagues, all of whom are listed in the acknowledgments in the front of the book.

Information Sources

Information in the narratives was derived from a variety of sources. Much of it comes from personal knowledge I've obtained in the field. My own experience in the LRGV includes hundreds of hours of observation at various times of the year, but especially during the fall months. Other information was derived from published accounts, all of which are noted in Appendix 2, References.

Additional information sources include: 1) personal discussions with several Valley residents and visitors; 2) reports of site visits by a number of individuals, most of which were submitted to TX-Butterfly

Digest; 3) annual Seasonal Summary lists from the Lepidopterist Society for 1994 to 2003; 4) annual July 4th Butterfly Counts, published by the North American Butterfly Association (NABA).

The Appendices

Appendix 1 is a glossary that defines the technical terms used in this book that might need further clarification. Many of these terms are also illustrated in Figure 1 (*page 4*). These terms are essential in describing butterfly characteristics. I have attempted to limit them to only those that are necessary.

Appendix 2 is References, a bibliography that lists all the publications mentioned in this book, as well as those utilized during my research. It also lists several comprehensive and regional field guides of interest. These works contain additional information about the butterflies that can considerably enhance your understanding of them. I encourage you to look beyond the information available in this single publication.

Appendix 3, Butterfly Checklist for the Lower Rio Grande Valley, includes all 282 species recorded in the LRGV to date, with the 153 LRGV specialties listed in boldface. It follows the taxonomic order established by NABA and uses that organization's common and scientific names. When the scientific names published by Opler and Warren (2002) differ, those names are included in brackets. In addition, the checklist gives an abundance status code for each species, as well as the months in which each has been recorded in the LRGV, if known. The checklist can be used to keep a personal record of the species you've observed within the LRGV.

The Lower Rio Grande Valley

The Lower Rio Grande Valley (LRGV) extends approximately 135 miles from Falcon Reservoir to the Gulf of Mexico. This unique corner of Texas is one of only two semitropical areas in the continental United States. The other is south Florida.

For the purposes of this book, the LRGV includes the Rio Grande floodplain and the land up to about twenty miles north, encompassing the three southernmost Texas counties of, from west to east, Starr, Hidalgo, and Cameron.

In several ways the LRGV is more like the semitropical areas of Mexico than anywhere north of the border. The climate, with mild winters and hot, humid summers, results in a rich diversity of plants and animals with a southern affinity, many of which do not occur farther north.

Once a wild and little-inhabited area, the LRGV now contains a chain of settlements, including several that have grown into large cities, and considerable agricultural acreage in orchards and other croplands. Only a few scattered remnants of natural landscapes remain, and increased urbanization, with its related highways, developments, and malls, continues to threaten what little natural character still exists.

Yet, those patches of native vegetation support some of America's rarest and most fascinating wildlife. To counteract the increasing sprawl, several federal, state, and non-governmental organizations have made impressive strides in protecting some natural sites and restoring others. The conservation efforts in the Valley have come under the umbrella of the "Wildlife Corridor" program, coordinated by the U.S. Fish and Wildlife Service. This ongoing program is intended eventually to provide protection to 132,500 acres (about four percent) of the LRGV. Newly acquired sites, which often connect with the region's established parks and refuges, are beginning to form an extensive and increasingly valuable chain of protected habitats throughout the length of the LRGV.

The Setting

The LRGV landscape is dominated by the Rio Grande floodplain, typically a broad, sandy bottomland with dense vegetation. The adjacent slightly higher terrain features a thorn-scrub environment and numerous arroyos. The drainages are often rugged and dry most of the year, but occasional rains produce runoff that often floods the lower areas. Such rains revitalize the floodplain and can result in colorful wildflower blooms.

Precipitation varies considerably throughout the LRGV, but annual totals tend to decrease the greater the distance from the Gulf. The eastern portion of the LRGV is truly semitropical in nature, but the western half, starting in upper Hidalgo County, is considerably drier. This more open thorn-scrub habitat, more properly known as "Tamaulipan Scrub," once contained extensive native grasslands. Several decades of grazing and the suppression of wildfires have altered the vegetation considerably. Today, this "South Texas Brushland" contains many more cactuses and a greater abundance of woody plants than it did before settlement. Anaqua, brasil, spiny hackberry, kidneywood, lotebrush, mesquite, shrubby blue sage, and Spanish dagger are now commonplace.

The lower Rio Grande floodplain itself is only a shadow of what it was when first viewed by Europeans in the 16th century. Sabal palms dominated much of the floodplain from near the mouth of the Rio Grande upriver as much as eighty miles, but only two groves remain today. Most of the floodplain habitats have undergone similar changes. Native woody plants still relatively common in protected areas include anaqua, cedar elm, coma, hackberries, ratama, soapberry, tepeguaje, Texas ebony, and willows. Some of the more important undergrowth species include Barbados-cherry, boneset, brasil, crucita, lantanas, and Turk's cap. Open areas on the floodplain often have large stands of asters, rattlebush, and seepwillow.

Butterfly Viewing Sites

Several sites within the LRGV region are well known by nature enthusiasts for the wildlife found within them. Although birders were the first to discover and take advantage of these choice sites, they are also rapidly being recognized for their butterfly diversity.

The best known of these varied sites, from east to west within the corridor, are Laguna Atascosa National Wildlife Refuge; Sabal Palm Audubon Center and Sanctuary; Weslaco's Valley Nature Center and Frontera Audubon Society Center; Santa Ana National Wildlife Refuge; Anzalduas County Park; Bentsen-Rio Grande Valley State Park; Rio Grande City's floodplain; Roma's miniature forest, just below the international bridge; and Falcon State Park, on the shore of Falcon Reservoir.

In recent years, several additional locales have become recognized as choice sites because of the potential they offer for finding many of the Valley's most-wanted butterflies. These sites include, from east to west, Boca Chica; South Padre Island Convention Center Garden; Palo Alto Battlefield National Historic Site, northeast of Brownsville; Los Ebanos Preserve at the junction of Expressway 88/83 and SH 100; Harlingen's Hugh Ramsey Nature Park; Longoria Wildlife Management Area near Santa Rosa; Golden Raintree Garden in Weslaco; Edinburg's World Birding Center; Lucy's Garden next to the Mission City Hall; Mission West RV Park; and the North American Butterfly Association's International Butterfly Park.

The map on pages 12–13 shows the general location of many of these sites. The following annotated list provides additional insight into the twenty key butterfly-viewing sites in the LRGV. From east to west, they include:

1. **Boca Chica.** This area near the mouth of the Rio Grande is accessible from US 77/83 in Brownsville via Boca Chica Boulevard (SH 4). The sandy landscape contains numerous Spanish daggers that are used by Yucca Giant-Skippers when they fly in March and April. The area is part of the Lower Rio Grande

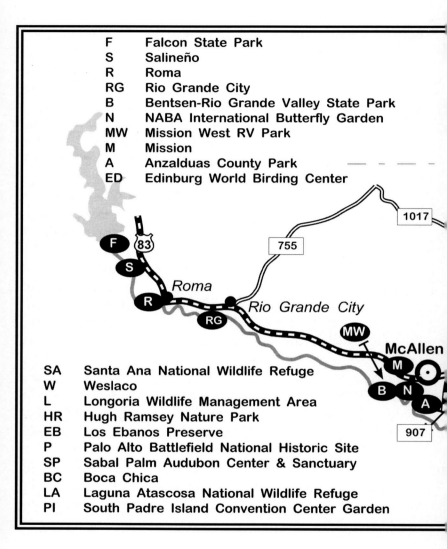

F   Falcon State Park
S   Salineño
R   Roma
RG   Rio Grande City
B   Bentsen-Rio Grande Valley State Park
N   NABA International Butterfly Garden
MW   Mission West RV Park
M   Mission
A   Anzalduas County Park
ED   Edinburg World Birding Center

SA   Santa Ana National Wildlife Refuge
W   Weslaco
L   Longoria Wildlife Management Area
HR   Hugh Ramsey Nature Park
EB   Los Ebanos Preserve
P   Palo Alto Battlefield National Historic Site
SP   Sabal Palm Audubon Center & Sanctuary
BC   Boca Chica
LA   Laguna Atascosa National Wildlife Refuge
PI   South Padre Island Convention Center Garden

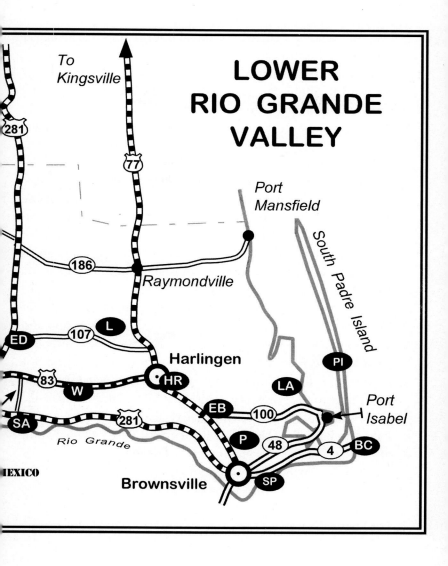

LOWER RIO GRANDE VALLEY

To Kingsville

281

77

Port Mansfield

186

Raymondville

South Padre Island

ED

107

L

Harlingen

83

HR

W

PI

LA

EB

100

Port Isabel

SA

281

P

48

4

BC

Rio Grande

MEXICO

Brownsville

SP

National Wildlife Refuge. Additional information is available at http://southwest.fws.gov/refuges/texas/lrgv.html/.

2. **South Padre Island Convention Center.** The center, located four miles north of the causeway exit onto the island, has a butterfly garden in front and on the south side of the building. Mangrove Buckeyes have been found here on occasion. From US 77, take SH 100 east approximately twenty-eight miles to the center. Additional information is available at www.spichamber.com/.

3. **Laguna Atascosa National Wildlife Refuge.** This 45,000-acre refuge (fee area) contains a marvelous butterfly garden at the visitor center, where thirty-two specialty butterflies have been recorded. From Rio Hondo, take FM 106 east to Buena Vista Rd. Turn left to the refuge. Additional information is available at http://southwest.fws.gov/refuges/texas/laguna.html.

4. **Sabal Palm Audubon Center and Sanctuary.** The preserve (fee area) is only 527 acres, but it has an excellent butterfly garden at the entrance and a network of trails through the palm grove and adjacent woodlands. A total of forty-three specialties have been recorded here. From US 77/83 north of Brownsville, take FM 511 south to FM 3068. Continue south to FM 1419 and go west about a half mile to the sanctuary. Additional information is available at www.audubon.org/local/sanctuary/sabal.

5. **Palo Alto Battlefield National Historic Site.** This 3,400-acre unit of the National Park Service is the most reliable site in the LRGV for Definite Patch. It is located northeast of Brownsville at the junction of FM 511 and FM 1847. Additional information is available at www.nps.gov/paal/.

6. **Los Ebanos Preserve.** Opened to the public in 2002, this private eighty-two-acre site (fee area) on SH 100, only 100 yards off US 77/83, has gardens surrounding the great house. A total of twenty-two specialties have been recorded so far, and it is one of the best sites for Mexican Bluewings. Additional information is available at www.losebanospreserve.com.

7. **Hugh Ramsey Nature Park.** This forty-acre tract is situated on the north side of Harlingen along the Arroyo Colorado off Ed Carey Drive (Loop 499) south of its intersection with FM 106. It has an extensive planted area. A total of twenty-five specialties have been recorded. Additional information is available at http://www.kiskadee.org/habitat.htm.

8. **Longoria Wildlife Management Area.** This management area, maintained by the Texas Parks and Wildlife Department, is situated along FM 506, eleven miles north of US 83. A network of trails provides good access to thorn-scrub habitat that is not as readily accessible elsewhere in the LRGV. Additional information is available at www.tpwd.state.tx.us/birdingtrails/lower/longoria/text.htm.

9. **Weslaco.** One of the very best butterfly-finding locations in the LRGV, the town contains three separate sites: Valley Nature Center (fee area) at 301 S. Border Street, Frontera Audubon Society Center (fee area) at 1101 S. Texas Blvd., and Golden Raintree Garden at 1303 S. Texas Blvd. A total of forty-three specialties have been recorded at those sites. Additional information is available at www.valleynaturecenter.org and www.fronteraaudubon.org.

10. **Santa Ana National Wildlife Refuge.** More specialty butterflies (sixty-one) have been recorded at this 2,088-acre refuge (fee area) than any other site in the LRGV. There are extensive butterfly gardens at the visitor center, along the entrance road, and along the first two miles of the seven-mile loop drive. Access is along US 281; go 7.5 miles south of US 83 on FM 907 from Alamo. Additional information is available at http://southwest.fws.gov/refuges/texas/santana.html.

11. **Edinburg World Birding Center.** Opened in 2003, this forty-acre site features an extensive butterfly garden and a network of trails. The number of specialties (eleven) seen here is sure to increase. The site is located in Edinburg. Take University Drive east from US 281 and turn south on Raul Longoria to Sprague St. Go east

to the center, on the left. Additional information is available at www.worldbirdingcenter.org/sites/edinburg/index.phtml.

12. **Mission.** The site of the annual Butterfly Festival each October, there are three small gardens that have produced an amazing number of butterflies. The new "Lucy's Garden" and Parks and Recreation Building garden are along 8th St., immediately west of Bryan Rd., just south of Bus. 83. The old "Lucy's Garden" is located behind the Kika La Garza Building, beyond the library on 12th St. Additional information is available at www.texasbutterfly.com.

13. **Anzalduas County Park.** One of the better-known birding sites, the park (fee on weekends) also has produced numerous butterflies of note in recent years. The best area lies across the dike to the east. The park is located off FM 494, two miles south of Expressway 83. Additional information is available at www.missionchamber.com/anzalduas.html.

14. **NABA International Butterfly Park.** Opened in 2003, its eighty-three acres are dominated by a series of butterfly gardens with a network of trails for easy access. Owned and operated by the North American Butterfly Association, at least one LRGV first-record butterfly, Aquamarine Hairstreak, has already been recorded. The garden is located off Old Military Highway (FM 494) one mile east of FM 2062, the entrance road to Bentsen-Rio Grande Valley State Park. Additional information is available at www.naba.org/nababp/.

15. **Bentsen-Rio Grande Valley State Park.** This 587-acre state park (fee area) has a butterfly garden and an extensive network of trails through the woodlands. No longer a choice birding site, due to the removal of the once popular "trailer loop," the garden has also declined. From US 83 west of Mission, take FM 2062 south to the park entrance. Additional information is available at www.tpwd.state.tx.us/park/bentsen/.

16. **Mission West RV Park.** This private RV park has a long hedge of duranta shrubs along the eastern border that can produce an

amazing variety of butterflies when flowering in fall. Although there is no charge to butterfly watchers, checking in at the office on arrival is required. The park is located south of Bus. 83, at 3805 West Bus. 83, between the Inspiration Road exit and FM 2062. Additional information is available at www.missionwestrv.com.

17. **Chihuahua Wood Preserve.** Owned and maintained by The Nature Conservancy, this 243-acre wildlife preserve west of Mission offers a diversity of habitats from cactus scrub to thorn forest. A one-mile trail provides easy access. A butterfly checklist is available. The site is located off Bus. 83, west of FM 1427. Where Bus. 83 turns northwest, go left .8 miles. Additional information is available at http://nature.org/wherewework/northamerica/states/texas/.

18. **Roma.** There is a small riparian area below the International Bridge at Roma that has produced numerous specialty butterflies over the years; Polydamas Swallowtail is regular here. Access is either from a side road to the north just before the bridge entrance or by steep cement stairs at Estrella Street Park, three blocks off US 83 via Lincoln Street. No website is available.

19. **Salineño.** Located along the Rio Grande and best known as a good place to find several avian specialties, the trails up- and downriver also offer good potential for finding a variety of specialty butterflies. Access is via a mostly paved roadway through town and past the "Birder's Colony" to the river. No website is available.

20. **Falcon State Park.** This state park (fee area) covers an area of 573 acres of desert-scrub habitat alongside Falcon Reservoir. Butterflies, principally those of the more arid areas in the western portion of the LRGV, can be abundant following spring and summer rainy periods. The adjacent countryside also offers good potential. Additional information is available at www.tpwd.state.tx.us/park/falcon.

A far more extensive discussion of the ten best areas in the LRGV, including comprehensive butterfly checklists for those sites, is included in my soon-to-be-published book, *Texas Butterfly Site Guide.*

The Butterflies

The 282 species of butterflies recorded within the LRGV represent nearly seventy percent of all known Texas species (about 425) and almost forty percent of all the species recorded in North America (about 730). There are more butterfly species in the LRGV than are found in the United States east of the Mississippi River.

Of the almost 300 LRGV species, more than half (153) are specialties, species that are unlikely to be found elsewhere in the United States. They are the ones that have given the LRGV its reputation as North America's most exciting butterfly-watching location. And they are the principal reason that increasing numbers of butterfly enthusiasts are attracted to the LRGV.

Almost every year, additional species are discovered in the LRGV, many of which are new to North American butterfly fauna. Three new records were added to the growing list of LRGV butterflies just in 2003 and early 2004: Mountain Groundstreak, Beautiful Beamer, and Pale Sicklewing. The latter two species were also new U.S. records. Whether these new discoveries are a result of global warming that is gradually providing more suitable conditions farther north, or simply the result of greater numbers of observers, the phenomenon has created considerable excitement within the community of butterfly enthusiasts.

Although a good diversity of butterflies can be expected in the LRGV year-round, with the exception of a few days each winter when extreme cold fronts from the north reach south Texas, the very best time of year is fall, October into December. That is when many of the new discoveries have occurred and when the rarest of the LRGV specialties are most likely to be seen.

Many of these most-wanted species are strays from Mexico. They may remain a few days or quickly move elsewhere. Although they can appear almost anywhere, the majority are reported from gardens or patches of flowering crucitas at scattered locations.

Taking advantage of the recent surge of interest in butterflies, the Mission Chamber of Commerce has sponsored a Texas Butterfly Festival (www.texasbutterfly.com) during the third week of October each year since 1996. This event attracts butterfly enthusiasts from throughout North America and Mexico and has become an important economic benefit to the region.

Participants can enjoy numerous field trips, led by experts, to all the best butterfly-viewing sites in the LRGV, as well as a wide variety of talks on topics ranging from butterfly identification to where to go to find specific species. More than 2,000 participants come to Mission each year. A total of 102 butterfly species were recorded during the 2003 festival.

Because the LRGV is America's number-one butterfly area, the North American Butterfly Association (NABA) has established the NABA International Butterfly Park (www.naba.org/nababp/) on the Rio Grande floodplain, next door to Bentsen-Rio Grande Valley State Park. This eighty-three-acre park, the first facility of its kind in the world, includes a series of gardens designed to attract butterflies and a network of maintained trails for the best viewing of them. Upon the completion of the park, with its abundant plant life, including larval foodplants as well as those utilized primarily as a nectar source, the NABA International Butterfly Park is destined to become the single most important butterfly-viewing site in North America.

Butterflies of the
Lower Rio Grande Valley

All the butterflies that have been recorded in the Lower Rio Grande Valley (LRGV), including historical reports, are described in this section. They are divided into the six butterfly families, using the taxonomy and nomenclature of the North American Butterfly Association. The vast majority are illustrated by photographs showing the most common view—upperside or underside. Both views are shown when appropriate and available.

Each species account includes a description, when and where they are most likely to be found, similar species, and additional pertinent remarks. The description begins with the most common view and ends with the wingspan. Technical terms are defined in Appendix 1, Glossary.

The when-and-where section provides a general statement of status, the months recorded when known, and where the species is most likely to be found. The terms used to describe the status are:

Abundant: many can be expected on most visits to appropriate locations.
Common: several can be expected on most visits to appropriate locations.
Uncommon: a few can often be found on most visits to appropriate locations.
Occasional: one or a very few can sometimes be found on visits to appropriate locations; usually reported every year.
Rare: one to several occur every few years only.
Accidental: a nonbreeding stray, may never be found again.
Historical: records prior to 1980 only.
Local: one to many are possible but normally only at specific locations.

LRGV specialties are indicated as such in the descriptions, and their names are also in **boldface** type when they are mentioned as a similar species in other accounts. A comprehensive checklist of LRGV butterflies is included in Appendix 3, with the names of the specialties also printed in **boldface** type.

Swallowtails— Family Papilionidae

Members of the swallowtail family in the LRGV are always large and usually showy. Most have a tail on each hindwing and three visible pairs of walking legs. Adults fly relatively slowly, generally five to seven feet above the ground, and all visit flowers for nectar. They constantly flutter their wings while feeding, and both sexes, but especially males, frequently sip water at puddles for nutrients. All typically perch with their wings spread.

Pipevine Swallowtail *Battus philenor*

A large, mostly black butterfly, the trailing portions of the upperside of the hindwings are iridescent blue-green, especially prominent on males. There is a series of white spots along the margins of both wings, more noticeable on females. The underside of the hindwing has a submarginal band of large orange spots and white marginal spots. Wingspan: 2.75–4 in.

When and Where: Widespread and common year-round. It frequents fields, roadsides, gardens, and occasionally woodland sites, feeding on a wide variety of flowering plants. Females sometimes hover low over the ground for long periods searching for low-growing pipevines, their larval foodplant.

Similar Species: The female Black Swallowtail (*page 26*) is most alike but has a small yellow spot on the leading edge of the upperside forewing near the apex and an orange-capped black spot on the inner margin of the hindwing. The rare, tailless **Polydamas Swallowtail** (*page 24*) can appear similar at a distance but lacks the iridescent blue and has a submarginal band of golden-yellow spots across both wings. The female **Broad-banded Swallowtail** (*page 33*) is similar but has short tails.

Remarks: This butterfly was named for the pipevine plant (*Aristolochia*), its larval foodplant. Pipevine plants contain aristolochic acid, which is ingested by the caterpillars. The acid causes Pipevine Swallowtail adults and larvae to be distasteful to predators. The red spots on the abdomen contain glands that emit an acrid odor when pinched.

Polydamas Swallowtail *Battus polydamas*

LRGV specialty. One of the tailless swallowtails, it is mostly coal-black on the upperside with a submarginal band of golden-yellow arrow-heads (pointed toward the head on both wings, larger on the hind-wings). The underside is paler, with a series of wavy red submarginal lines on the hindwings. Wingspan: 3–4 in.

When and Where: Widespread but occasional, from March to January. Most sightings are at wild olives or flowering shrubs in gardens. Larval foodplants are pipevines.

Similar Species: Pipevine (*page 22*) and small male Black (*page 26*) swallowtails are similar, because they are mostly black. Both have tails and neither has the distinctive golden-yellow submarginal band.

Remarks: An earlier and very appropriate name for this well-marked swallowtail was "Gold Rim."

Dark Kite-Swallowtail *Eurytides philolaus*

LRGV specialty. Its blackish-brown and white pattern and extremely long tails are distinctive. The upperside has a white median band across both wings, white lines between the band and leading edge of the forewing, a submarginal band of white lines, and red spots on the inner edge of the hindwing. The underside is similar. Wingspan: 2.5–3.5 in.

When and Where: Accidental, recorded only a few times in July and October. Since it is fairly common in nearby Mexico, additional sightings are possible. Larval foodplants include members of the Annonaceae family, such as pawpaw, which do not occur in the LRGV.

Similar Species: No other LRGV butterfly is similar; it most resembles the Zebra Swallowtail of the eastern United States, which does not occur in the LRGV.

Remarks: A Dark Kite-Swallowtail was recorded on the 2003 July 4th Butterfly Count at Bentsen-Rio Grande Valley State Park.

Black Swallowtail *Papilio polyxenes*

Sexually dimorphic, males are mostly black with two bands of yellow spots across both wings; the arrowhead-shaped submarginal spots are larger than those on the margins. Females have smaller and paler marginal spots, as well as a series of prominent blue postmedian spots across the hindwings. Both have a lone yellow spot on the leading edge of the forewing near the apex and an orange-capped black spot on the inner margin of the hindwing. The underside is black with yellow-orange median and yellowish submarginal spot-bands and a pale cell spot on the hindwing. Wingspan: 2.75–3.75 in.

When and Where: Widespread but uncommon year-round. It prefers open, rather than wooded, areas, but in hilly places (rare in the LRGV), males frequent hilltops to search for females. Larval foodplants include various members of the Umbelliferae family, including dill, parsley, and carrots.

Similar Species: Pipevine Swallowtail (*page 22*) is similar to the female Black but lacks the yellow spot on the forewing upperside and the orange-capped black spot on the hindwing. **Polydamas Swallowtail** (*page 24*), which is tailless and has a golden-yellow submarginal band, also has similar features. The female **Broad-banded Swallowtail** (*page 33*) is somewhat similar but has short tails.

Remarks: Female Black Swallowtails are said to mimic Pipevine Swallowtails, which are distasteful to predators.

Thoas Swallowtail *Papilio thoas*

LRGV specialty. Very similar to a faded Giant Swallowtail, the Thoas is blackish-brown with pale-yellow spot-bands that form an X near the wingtip. The median spots are somewhat square. The pale-yellow underside has a dark median band with blue crescents. Wingspan: 4–5.5 in.

When and Where: Accidental, from April to July and in September and October. This species is fairly common in nearby Mexico, so additional sightings are possible. Larval foodplants include citrus trees, pricklyash, and pipers.

Similar Species: The common Giant Swallowtail (*page 30*) is most alike; fresh individuals have brighter yellow wing bands. The spots on the bands are rounded and uniform on the Thoas and pointed and irregularly shaped on the Giant. Ornythion Swallowtail (*page 32*) is also similar, but its yellow bands do not cross to form an X near the wingtip. Ornythion tails are solid black.

Remarks: The shape and uniformity of the pale-yellow bands must be studied carefully for identification. Records are probably based on close examination of collected specimens.

Giant Swallowtail *Papilio cresphontes*

The largest of the common North American butterflies, its upperside is dark-brown to black with a diagonal band of yellow spots that extends from wingtip to wingtip across the abdomen. It has a second submarginal band with smaller spots. The yellow bands meet near the tip of the forewing to form an X. A red-capped black spot is present on the inner margin of each hindwing, and the tails are yellow with black margins. The underside is pale yellow with a postmedian line of black, blue, and red patches and a red-rimmed black tailspot on the hindwing. Wingspan: 3.5–5 in.

When and Where: Widespread and common year-round. It frequents open areas, as well as woodland sites, and spends considerable time feeding in gardens. Larval foodplants include various citrus trees, such as grapefruit and orange—common in the LRGV—as well as pricklyash.

Similar Species: The very rare **Thoas Swallowtail** (*page 28*) is most alike. See the discussion in its account regarding the difficulty in separating these two species. The rare Ornython Swallowtail male (*page 32*) also has a pair of pale-yellow wing bands, but they do not meet to form an X near the wingtip. Its tail is solid black. The **Broad-banded Swallowtail** (*page 33*), a rare stray, has an extremely broad yellow wing band; its tail is solid black.

Remarks: Giant Swallowtail caterpillars are locally known as "Orange Dogs."

Swallowtails—Family Papilionidae

Ornythion Swallowtail *Papilio ornythion*

The two pale-yellow wing bands—a broad median band that extends from wingtip to wingtip and a parallel submarginal band, including five large chevrons on the hindwing—do not meet near the apex to form an X. The yellow bands are reduced or obscured on females. The tail is solid black. The underside is similar with several red triangles within a broad, brown postmedian band, and an extensive brown basal patch with yellow streaks. Wingspan: 3.25–4.5 in.

When and Where: Widespread but rare, from March to June and August to November. Most sightings are along the edges of wooded areas, including orchards. Larval foodplants consist of various citrus trees, both agricultural and ornamental.

Similar Species: Giant Swallowtail (*page 30*) and **Thoas Swallowtail** (*page 28*) are most alike, but their yellow wing bands meet near the wingtips to form an X, and their tails are black with a yellow center.

Remarks: Spotting this swallowtail is serendipitous; it can never be expected.

Broad-banded Swallowtail *Papilio astyalus*

LRGV specialty. Sexually dimorphic, males show a very wide yellow median band, a separate yellow spot within the forewing cell, and a series of large yellow submarginal crescents on the hindwing. Females are blackish-brown with similar yellow submarginal crescents on the hindwing, but they have an additional postmedian row of blue crescents. They also have a row of thin yellow submarginal spots on the forewing. Males have long black tails, but females have only a stub. Wingspan: 4–4.75 in.

When and Where: Accidental, in April and from August to October. This species is fairly common in adjacent Mexico, so additional sightings are possible. Most likely to be seen in and around orchards of citrus trees, their larval foodplant, but Neck states that "females stay in wooded areas … males fly in open areas."

Similar Species: No other swallowtail has as wide a wing band as the males. The mostly dark females could initially be confused with Pipevine (*page 22*) or Black (*page 26*) swallowtails, but those species have long tails.

Remarks: No other LRGV swallowtail has such obvious sexual dimorphism.

Three-tailed Swallowtail *Papilio pilumnus*

LRGV specialty. A relatively small, black-and-yellow swallowtail with three tails on each hindwing. The upperside has yellow "tiger stripes" on the basal half, a broad black postmedian band with blue patches near the tails, and a series of yellow submarginal lines. The underside is brown with a similar pattern. Wingspan: 3.75–4 in.

When and Where: Accidental, a single historical sighting in May. Since it does occur in nearby Mexico, additional sightings are possible. Larval foodplants are unknown.

Similar Species: Eastern Tiger Swallowtail (*page 332*) is most alike but is only hypothetical in the LRGV.

Remarks: In Mexico, this species occurs in forested mountain areas.

Magnificent Swallowtail *Papilio garamas*

LRGV specialty. A gorgeous, coal-black swallowtail, the Magnificent has a broad yellow median band that forms a wide U across both wings, a narrow band of yellow crescents across the forewing, deeply scalloped hindwings, and short black tails. The underside is also spectacular, with a yellow median band that has long "teeth" tipped with orange. Wingspan: 3.5–4.25 in.

When and Where: Accidental, historical records only from September and October following a hurricane in the 1960s. Since this species does occur in nearby Mexico, additional sightings are possible. Larval foodplants are unknown, although it likely utilizes citrus trees.

Similar Species: No other swallowtail has a broad yellow band that forms a wide U-pattern across coal-black wings. Female Magnificent Swallowtails could initially be confused with Pipevines (*page 22*), but they lack any yellow markings on the upperside.

Remarks: Some authors refer to this species as "Abderus Swallowtail" after its subspecific name, *abderus*.

Pink-spotted Swallowtail *Papilio pharnaces*

LRGV specialty. The upperside of this large swallowtail is mostly blackish-brown with two rows of pink spots on the deeply serrated hindwings and white marginal crescents; it may sometimes be tailless. The underside is similar. Wingspan: 3.5–3.75 in.

When and Where: Accidental, one record in April. It is uncommon in nearby Mexico, but additional sightings are possible. Larval food-plants in Mexico include citrus foliage.

Similar Species: **Ruby-spotted Swallowtail** (*page 37*) is similar but has a single row of red spots on the hindwing.

Remarks: Because of the abundance of citrus in the LRGV, it is strange that the Pink-spotted isn't more numerous.

Ruby-spotted Swallowtail *Papilio anchisiades*

LRGV specialty. The wings of this tailless swallowtail are coal black (slightly paler toward the wingtips), except for a row of large red ovals and smaller red spots on the hindwings. Several tiny, red thorax spots are visible on the underside. Wingspan: 2.75–4 in.

When and Where: Rare and local, from April to July and September to December. It does not occur every year. It frequents woodland areas and feeds on adjacent flowering plants. It frequently rests in shaded areas. Larval foodplants consist of various citrus trees.

Similar Species: The similar **Pink-spotted Swallowtail** (*page 36*) has been recorded on one occasion. It has a double row of pink spots, rather than one row of red patches, on the trailing edge of the hindwing.

Remarks: Several eggs and larvae were found on jopoy leaves at Santa Ana NWR in 2003. It is known to wander as far north as Kansas.

Whites and Sulphurs—
Family Pieridae

Members of this family are small to medium in size, lack fully developed tails, and have three visible pairs of walking legs with forked claws. Flight is steady and often in a straight line. All normally perch with their wings held upright.

Whites—Subfamily Pierinae

Whites are predominately white in color, as their name suggests, but nearly all feature dark or black spots, bars, or other markings. Some species have areas of yellow wash on the wings. Whites of the LRGV utilize plants in the mustard family as larval foodplants.

Florida White *Appias drusilla*

LRGV specialty. The underside is satiny white with a faint yellow forewing base. The upperside of males is also satiny white with swollen veins. Females have dull-white forewings with brown wingtips; their hindwings show a yellowish wash. The antennae clubs are pale. Wingspan: 2–2.5 in.

When and Where: Occasional, from March to May and July to November. Most sightings are at flowering shrubs in wooded areas and adjacent gardens. Larval foodplants are limited to capers.

Similar Species: **Giant White** (*page 44*) is most alike, but both sexes have a black central spot on the forewing.

Remarks: Also known as "Tropical White" for its southern affinity. However, strays have been recorded as far north as Nebraska and New York.

Mountain White *Leptophobia aripa*

LRGV specialty. This relatively large butterfly is shell-white above and below, except for a tiny black center dot on the hindwing underside. The upperside has black wingtips and narrow black forewing margins. The antennae are banded, and the eyes are green. Wingspan: 2.5–2.75 in.

When and Where: Accidental, a lone October record. Because it is common in nearby Mexico, additional sightings are possible. Larval foodplants are unknown.

Similar Species: **Florida White** (*page 39*) is most similar but lacks a black hindwing spot and black wingtips.

Remarks: In Mexico this species resides in mountain forests, so the LRGV record is most unusual.

Whites—Subfamily Pierinae

Checkered White *Pontia protodice*

The only LRGV white that is marked with a checkered pattern of blackish-brown squares on the upperside. The male's hindwings are white; the female's hindwings show gray hourglass markings. The underside is faintly checkered on males; on females, underwings have a network of olive lines. Flight is usually fast, erratic, and low to the ground; it stops often to feed. Wingspan: 1.25–2 in.

When and Where: Common in open areas year-round. It is most numerous in weedy fields where various mustards, its larval foodplants, grow.

Male

Similar Species: The slightly larger Great Southern White (*page 43*) can be confused with Checkered Whites in flight, but a good view of the Great Southern White's upperside will readily reveal white wings with only jagged dark marginal markings. In northern Texas, Checkered Whites are sometimes confused with Cabbage Whites (*page 42*), a very rare stray to the LRGV that has black center spots on the forewing.

Male

Remarks: Checkered Whites can be abundant in fields and pastures. When disturbed, they remain in the open rather than seeking cover.

Female

Cabbage White *Pieris rapae*

The upperside is snow white with a single black center spot on the male's forewing and two black center spots on the female's. Both show dark wingtips. The underside can be pure white or have a yellowish wash. Wingspan: 1.5–2.25 in.

When and Where: Accidental in the LRGV, from October to December, but common throughout most of the United States.

Similar Species: Checkered White (*page 41*) is most alike, but it has numerous brown forewing spots and jagged brown marginal markings on the upperside and yellow veining on the underside.

Remarks: Because of its abundance throughout the northern states and rarity in the LRGV, visitors from northern areas should look twice at any individual assumed to be this species.

Great Southern White *Ascia monuste*

A medium-sized butterfly, the Great Southern is sexually dimorphic. Males have an all-white upperside, except for jagged black forewing margins. Females are washed with pale brown and have a brown forewing spot. The underside is white on males, but it is clouded with darker veins on females. The antennae clubs are fluorescent blue. Wingspan: 1.75–2.5 in.

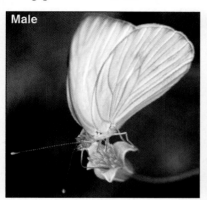
Male

Female

When and Where: Widespread and common year-round. Most abundant near the Gulf Coast, where it uses saltwort as its larval foodplant. It is less numerous inland but regularly visits gardens and roadside wildflowers.

Similar Species: Florida White (*page 39*) is most alike and of comparable size, but lacks the jagged dark margins. The larger **Giant White** (*page 44*) has a single black forewing spot.

Remarks: Great Southern Whites can be very abundant on the coastal prairies in spring.

Giant White *Ganyra josephina*

LRGV specialty. This large white has a contrasting black spot near the leading edge of the forewing. Males are bright white, due to chalk-white scales, but females show a brownish wash with three brownish spots just below the black spot. Wing margins are unmarked on males, but those of females have a faint jagged brown edge. The underside is identical. Wingspan: 2.5–4 in.

When and Where: Widespread but occasional, from March to January, with most sightings from September to December. Most often encountered in gardens where wandering individuals stop to feed. Larval foodplants include capers.

Similar Species: Although the smaller Cabbage White (*page 42*) is similar, both males and females show dark wingtips. Great Southern White (*page 43*) and **Florida White** (*page 39*) are smaller and lack the Giant's black forewing spot. The very rare **Mountain White** (*page 40*) is smaller and has broad black wingtips.

Remarks: The largest white found north of Mexico, it is a Mexican species that normally occurs in the United States only in the LRGV.

Falcate Orangetip *Anthocharis midea*

This small white is sexually dimorphic. Males have orange on the upperside of their slightly falcate wingtips; females lack the orange wingtips. Forewings of both are primarily white with a dark spot near the leading edge and black-and-white checkered margins. The underside of the hindwing is white with a lace-like pattern that ranges from black to gold, darker on males. Wingspan: 1.25–1.5 in.

When and Where: Occasional, from February to April. This white is most likely to be seen in open areas and in flight. It stops rarely to feed on low-growing wildflowers. Larval foodplants include a few wetland mustards, such as bittercress and pepperweed.

Similar Species: No other small, primarily white butterfly in the LRGV has orange wingtips.

Remarks: One of the earliest of the "springtime" butterflies, it isn't seen after April.

Male

Female

Sulphurs—Subfamily Coliadinae

Sulphurs are predominantly yellow, but some members also show brown, black, green, and white. Sulphurs utilize plants of the legume (Fabaceae) family as larval foodplants.

Orange Sulphur   *Colias eurytheme*

Orange Sulphurs are medium-sized, yellow to dusky-orange butterflies. Females can be whitish-green. The underside features a pair of red-rimmed silver spots in the center of the hindwing, a series of widely spaced brown submarginal spots, and a dark spot near the leading edge of the forewing. The upperside has wide dark margins, darker on males, and a single black spot near the leading edge of the forewing. Wingtips are slightly rounded. Wingspan: 1.75–2.5 in.

When and Where: Widespread but uncommon year-round. It prefers open areas, and only rarely frequents shaded sites. Larval foodplants include a wide assortment of legumes, such as clover and alfalfa.

Similar Species: Southern Dogface (*page 48*) is most alike, but its wingtips are pointed rather than rounded. Several other medium-sized sulphurs—Lyside Sulphur (*page 56*), Mexican Yellow (*page 60*), and Sleepy Orange (*page 66*)—share some similarities but lack the underside spots.

Remarks: Orange Sulphur was earlier known as "Alfalfa Butterfly," due to its affinity for alfalfa fields in other areas of the country.

Sulphurs—Subfamily Coliadinae

Southern Dogface *Colias cesonia*

The dog-face pattern on the upperside of the male's forewing, complete with a large black eye with a silver center, is most evident when it's perched with open wings but is also evident, if backlit, when it's perched with closed wings. The dog-face pattern is less defined on females. Overall, the Dogface is bright yellow to yellow-green, although females are rarely whitish. Both sexes have pink on the wing margins and pointed wingtips. Wingspan: 1.75–2.5 in.

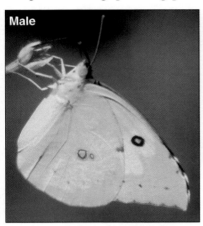

Male

Female

When and Where: Widespread and usually common year-round. It is more numerous in open areas and along wooded edges than in shaded locations. It commonly visits gardens, as well. Larval foodplants consist of a wide assortment of legumes, including Texas kidneywood.

Similar Species: Orange Sulphur (*page 46*) is most alike but has rounded wingtips and is generally smaller.

Remarks: Sometimes known as "Dogface" or "Dogface Butterfly," this species often drinks at puddles.

White Angled-Sulphur *Anteos clorinde*

LRGV specialty. This large sulphur, with a sharply angled shape and falcate wingtips, is leaf-green on the underside with bulging veins and a faint reddish spot on both wings. The upperside is white with a large orange-yellow patch on the leading edge of the forewing, most evident on males. Both sexes show a small black forewing spot. Wingspan: 2.75–3.5 in.

When and Where: Occasional, with records from most months. Seen from March to May, but the majority of sightings occur from July to January. Most often seen in flight, which is usually swift and high above the canopy. Larval foodplants are limited to *Cassia* species.

Similar Species: **Yellow Angled-Sulphur** (*page 50*) is most alike but is larger and typically has a yellow, rather than white, upperside.

Remarks: Known as "Clorinde" in some field guides, occasional individuals wander northward in late summer and fall.

Yellow Angled-Sulphur *Anteos maerula*

LRGV specialty. This angle-winged sulphur is even larger than the White Angled-Sulphur. The underside is leaf-green with a single whitened vein and a reddish oblong forewing spot. The upperside is bright yellow on males and dull yellow to white on females. Both sexes show a small black forewing spot. Wingspan: 3.75–4.5 in.

When and Where: Occasional, from February to December. It is found most frequently in flight, often high above the vegetation. Flight is usually fast and direct. Larval foodplants are limited to *Cassia* species.

Similar Species: **White Angled-Sulphur** (*page 49*) is most alike but has a large orange-yellow patch on the leading edge of its white forewing. Orange-barred Sulphur (*page 52*) is noticeably smaller with extensive reddish markings on the underside.

Male

Remarks: Like the White Angled-Sulphur, this sulphur is known to wander northward in late summer and fall. An earlier name for this tropical species was "Yellow Brimstone."

Sulphurs—Subfamily Coliadinae

Cloudless Sulphur *Phoebis sennae*

One of the large sulphurs, sexually dimorphic, and varied in pattern and color. Males are usually clear lemon-yellow on the underside, but they may have a pair of pink-rimmed silver patches on both wings. Females are yellow to greenish-yellow with a pair of pink-rimmed silver patches on the hindwing and a pair of rusty patches on the forewing. Both wings also have scattered reddish streaks. The upper-side is unmarked on males, but there is a reddish spot near the leading edge of the female's forewing. Flight is strong and direct, with sudden stops at feeding sites. Wingspan: 2.25–3 in.

Male

When and Where: Widespread and often abundant year-round. It can occur almost anywhere, from the Rio Grande floodplain into the Tamaulipan scrub habitat. It is also commonly found feeding on flowering plants in gardens. Larval foodplants are limited to legumes, including *Cassia* species.

Similar Species: Larger than Orange Sulphur, Southern Dogface, and other medium-sized sulphurs, it is most like the Large Orange Sulphur (*page 53*), which is marked with a straight submarginal line on the forewing. Orange-barred Sulphur (*page 52*) is larger, far less numerous, and has extensive red-orange markings. Also, the very rare **Statira Sulphur** (*page 55*) is similar but lacks any markings on the underside.

Remarks: Their lemon-yellow color can help identify males in flight, even at a distance.

Female

Sulphurs—Subfamily Coliadinae

Orange-barred Sulphur *Phoebis philea*

One of the largest of the LRGV sulphurs, it is sexually dimorphic. Males are mostly yellow on the underside, while the slightly larger females can be reddish-orange to whitish-yellow. Both sexes have a pair of small, black-rimmed, pale spots on the underside of both wings, along with a scattering of reddish and blackish streaks. The upperside is mostly yellow to orange with considerable reddish on the outer half of the hindwing, varying by sex. Males are yellowish with a large red-orange patch on the leading edge of the forewing. Females are orange-yellow with numerous black apical spots and black wingtips. The trailing half of the female's hindwing is reddish. Wingspan: 2.75–3.75 in.

When and Where: Uncommon and local, in April and from July to January. Likely sites include the Valley Nature Center and Sabal Palm Grove. Larval foodplants are limited to *Cassia* species. Flight is usually swift, but when feeding, they often can be closely approached for observation and photographs.

Similar Species: Most likely to be confused with the slightly smaller Large Orange Sulphur (*page 53*), which lacks the extensive reddish coloration and the red-orange patch on the forewing. Two other large sulphurs—**White Angled-Sulphur** (*page 49*) and **Yellow Angled-Sulphur** (*page 50*)—can be separated by their angled wings and leaf-green underside.

Remarks: This is a powerful flier, and a few individuals stray northward in late summer.

Sulphurs—Subfamily Coliadinae

Large Orange Sulphur *Phoebis agarithe*

Most individuals have an unbroken diagonal line from the wingtip through the center of the forewing, usually easily visible on the underside when perched. Sexually dimorphic, males are orange to yellow on the underside; females can be pale orange to dull white with scattered rusty and blackish spots and double black-rimmed, silver spots in the center of the hindwing. The upperside is all orange to orange-yellow on males and paler with a reddish forewing spot on females. Flight is usually swift and somewhat erratic. Wingspan: 2.25–2.5 in.

When and Where: Widespread and common year-round. Often the Valley's most abundant large sulphur, present in a wide diversity of habitats, ranging from weedy fields to woodlands, as well as in gardens. Larval foodplants include numerous members of the legume family, such as *Cassia* species and Texas ebony.

Male

Similar Species: Most like the larger and less common Orange-barred Sulphur (*page 52*), which lacks the diagonal line. The Large Orange Sulphur can also be confused with Cloudless Sulphur (*page 51*), which may have a broken, not straight, diagonal line on the forewing. The larger **White Angled-Sulphur** (*page 49*) and **Yellow Angled-Sulphur** (*page 50*) have angled wings and are leaf-green on the underside.

Remarks: This species often wanders northward throughout Texas and adjacent states in summer and fall.

Tailed Sulphur *Phoebis neocypris*

LRGV specialty. A large, sexually dimorphic species that has a short, tail-like extension on the hindwing. The underside of males is yellow-orange with scattered red spots and a pair of black-rimmed white spots on the hindwing and one large and one small black-rimmed white spot on the forewing. Females are variable from yellow to white with scattered reddish spots below. The upperside is mostly unmarked except for an orange central patch on males; females have dark margins. Wingspan: 1.5–1.75 in.

When and Where: Accidental, with records in October and November. Additional records are possible. Larval foodplants include senna.

Similar Species: Orange-barred (*page 52*) and Cloudless (*page 51*) sulphurs have similar spots on the underside but lack the tail-like extension.

Remarks: The Tailed Sulphur is rare in the mountainous areas of Mexico, south to Central America.

Statira Sulphur *Phoebis statira*

LRGV specialty. The underside is pale yellowish-green and unmarked, although the veins may be slightly swollen. The upperside shows sexual dimorphism. Males are clear yellow; female forewings are yellow with a dark spot and narrow dark apical margins. Wingspan: 2.75–3 in.

When and Where: Accidental, in February and June. Fairly common in nearby Mexico, so additional sightings are possible. Larval foodplants include calliandra and senna.

Similar Species: Cloudless Sulphur (*page 51*) is most alike, particularly the lemon-yellow males, but Statira Sulphurs lack any markings on the underside. Lyside Sulphur (*page 56*) can also be yellow-green but is considerably smaller.

Remarks: Sometimes referred to as "Embossed Sulphur," it is known for huge population movements in the tropics.

Lyside Sulphur *Kricognia lyside*

Overall color can be extremely variable, from a dull green or yellow to almost white. The one constant is a yellow or golden wing base, sometimes evident in flight. The underside of the hindwing usually has a satiny sheen and a noticeably thick median vein. Wing shape is almost triangular with pointed wingtips. Lyside Sulphurs are fast fliers, suddenly dropping onto a perch, often on the underside of a leaf or similar partly concealed site. Wingspan: 1.5–2.25 in.

When and Where: Widespread and abundant year-round. It can be very abundant after a particularly good emergence. Although it can be expected almost anywhere from the floodplain into the Tamaulipan scrub habitat, it is usually most numerous in the latter area where guayacan, its larval foodplant, is abundant.

Similar Species: **Statira Sulphur** (*page 55*) is similar but considerably larger. Boisduval's (*page 59*) and Mexican (*page 60*) yellows and Tailed Orange (*page 62*) are similar in size, but none of these have clear wings with a golden base.

Remarks: Because of its use of guayacan as a larval foodplant, this butterfly was once known as "Guayacan Sulphur."

Barred Yellow *Eurema daira*

Seasonally dimorphic, the underside is whitish-gray in summer. In winter it is yellow, with a fine sprinkling of reddish-brown. The upperside is yellow with broad brown wingtips and margins. It also has a broad dark bar along the inner margin of the male's forewing, pale and reduced on females and on winter forms. Wingspan: 1–1.5 in.

Summer

Winter

When and Where: Accidental, from August to November. It may be more common than the few records suggest, since it can easily be mistaken for a Little Yellow, especially females in flight. Larval foodplants consist of various members of the pea family, including bur-clover, mimosa, senna, and tickclover.

Similar Species: Little Yellow (*page 63*) is most alike but has two small, black basal spots on the underside of the hindwing. The upperside of the Dainty Sulphur (*page 67*) is somewhat like the female Barred Yellow but lacks the dark hindwing margins.

Remarks: This tropical species is not considered a LRGV specialty because it is also a resident of the southeastern states of Mississippi, Alabama, Georgia, South Carolina, and Florida.

Ghost Yellow *Eurema albula*

LRGV specialty. Sexually dimorphic, the male's underside is white with a faint yellowish wash and numerous swollen veins. The female's underside is similar but with scattered dark spots. The upperside is snow white except for black wingtips. The eyes are yellow and the legs are pale. Wingspan: .75–1 in.

When and Where: Accidental, with one November record. It occurs in nearby Mexico, so additional sightings are possible. Larval food-plants are unknown.

Similar Species: Barred Yellow males (*page 57*) are similar to Ghost Yellow males on the underside, but they have a broad dark inner-forewing margin. Little Yellow females (*page 63*) can also be whitish and spotted on the underside, but they have two tiny black basal spots.

Remarks: This little sulphur is also known as "Yellow White" and "Small White."

Boisduval's Yellow *Eurema boisduvaliana*

A medium-sized sulphur with an angled taillike protrusion on the hindwing. The underside is dull yellow with a curved rusty patch on the hindwing. The upperside has broad black margins on both wings, more extensive on males than females. Wingspan: 1.5–2 in.

When and Where: Uncommon and local, from April to January. It frequents shaded areas and is rarely missed in fall at Sabal Palm Grove and Los Ebanos Preserve. Larval foodplants include various *Cassia* species.

Similar Species: Mexican Yellow (*page 60*) and Sleepy Orange (*page 66*) are similar, but they have a straight rusty hindwing patch. The winter form of Tailed Orange (*page 62*) is also similar but is orange instead of yellow.

Remarks: Two populations of this tropical butterfly occur in the United States, one in the LRGV and a western population ranging from the Texas Big Bend Country to Arizona.

Mexican Yellow *Eurema mexicana*

A medium-sized, pale-yellow to creamy-white sulphur with an angled hindwing. Males are brighter yellow. The hindwing has rusty dusting and a long straight rusty patch on the underside. The upperside has black hindwing margins and a heavy black-and-white pattern on the forewing resembling an eyeless dog's face. It often appears white in flight, which is usually slow and low to the ground. Wingspan: 1.5–2 in.

When and Where: Widespread but rare, with records from every month. Most sightings are along trails and woodland edges. Larval foodplants consist of a variety of legumes, including acacias and *Cassia* species.

Similar Species: Boisduval's Yellow (*page 59*) is most alike but is brighter yellow and has a curved rusty patch on the hindwing. Tailed Orange (*page 62*), especially the winter form, is also similar but is orange instead of yellow and lacks the long rusty patch on the underside of the hindwing. The rare **Salome Yellow** (*page 61*) is similar but has a rusty hindwing spot.

Remarks: It was once known as "Wolf-faced Sulphur," due to the dog-face pattern on the forewing.

Sulphurs—Subfamily Coliadinae

Salome Yellow *Eurema salome*

LRGV specialty. This medium-sized, bright-yellow butterfly has an angled wing with a stub of a tail. The underside of the hindwing has numerous rusty markings, including scattered streaks and a round spot near the trailing edge. The upperside is bright yellow with a rusty apical area; the hindwing margin is also rusty on males. Wingspan: 1.50–2 in.

When and Where: Accidental, with a lone historical record in September. Since this species occurs in nearby Mexico, additional sightings are possible. Larval foodplants are unknown.

Similar Species: Mexican Yellow (*page 60*) is most alike but is paler and lacks the large, round, rusty hindwing spot.

Remarks: This species is sometimes known as "Monkey Face Sulphur."

Tailed Orange *Eurema proterpia*

Another of the medium-sized sulphurs, the Tailed Orange is seasonally dimorphic. The underside of the summer form is clear yellow-orange with a rounded hindwing; the winter form shows a scattering of rusty streaks and patches and an angled hindwing. The upperside is deep-orange to orange-yellow, with black on the leading edge of the forewing and wingtip. Wingspan: 1.5–2.25 in.

Summer

Winter

When and Where: Widespread but uncommon and sporadic in occurrence, from June to January. It utilizes a wide variety of habitats, from woodland edges to brushy fields. Larval foodplants include members of the pea family, such as mesquite and senna.

Similar Species: Sleepy Orange (*page 66*) is most alike but has a distinct rusty line on the underside of the hindwing. Boisduval's (*page 59*) and Mexican (*page 60*) yellows are somewhat alike, but both are paler and have a rusty line on the underside of the hindwing.

Remarks: Like a few other sulphurs, Tailed Orange wanders northward in late summer and fall. In spite of its name, only the winter form, which can occur as early as September, has the distinct tail-like projection of the hindwing.

Sulphurs—Subfamily Coliadinae

Little Yellow *Eurema lisa*

One of the small sulphurs, its color can vary from bright yellow or orange-yellow to almost white for females. The underside has scattered markings, including a large rusty spot near the upper edge and two tiny, black basal spots, both on the hindwing and evident only when perched. The upperside has broad black wingtips. Males also have narrow black hindwing margins. Flight is usually erratic and low, often among weeds and brush, as it progresses along roadsides and trail edges. Wingspan: 1–1.5 in.

Male

Female

When and Where: Widespread and common year-round. It is especially abundant in weedy areas along roadsides and in fields. Larval foodplants consist of a wide variety of legumes, including senna.

Similar Species: Mimosa Yellow (*page 64*) is most alike but lacks the two tiny, black basal spots on the hindwing. Two similar but very rare sulphurs are Barred Yellow (*page 57*) and Dina Yellow (*page 65*). Barred Yellow has a white summer form and a yellow winter form (with a rusty wash), but neither Barred nor Dina has the two black basal spots on the underside of the hindwing. **Ghost Yellow** (*page 58*) is similar to Little Yellow females but lacks the two underside basal spots.

Remarks: There are times when thousands of Little Yellows are present, flying low over grassy areas.

Mimosa Yellow *Eurema nise*

LRGV specialty. The underside of this little yellow sulphur shows reddish spots and streaks like the Little Yellow, but the hindwing base lacks the two tiny, black spots. The upperside has a wide black wingtip. Flight is seldom in the open; it is usually low within brushy areas. Wingspan: 1–1.25 in.

When and Where: Uncommon and local, from August to January. It frequents shaded areas in and adjacent to woodlands and is rarely found in the open. Larval foodplants are limited to mimosas.

Similar Species: Little Yellow (*page 63*) is most alike but has two tiny, black basal spots on the underside of the hindwing.

Remarks: When Mimosa Yellows do occur in open areas, they immediately retreat to shaded areas when disturbed. The species is sometimes known as "Blacktip Sulphur" because of its black wingtip.

Dina Yellow *Eurema dina*

Another of the small yellow sulphurs with scattered rusty patches and spots, including a single dark basal spot on the underside of the hindwing. The upperside is orange-yellow with very narrow apical margins, black on males and reddish on females. Wingspan: 1.25–2 in.

When and Where: Accidental, recorded only in April, July, and September. Fairly common in nearby Mexico, so additional sightings are possible. Larval foodplants are limited to allthorn and tree of heaven.

Similar Species: Little Yellow (*page 63*) is similar but has two tiny, black basal spots on the underside of the hindwing.

Remarks: This Mexican species also occurs in southern Florida and southern Arizona.

Sleepy Orange *Eurema nicippe*

This medium-sized sulphur has a slightly angled hindwing and is seasonally dimorphic. Summer forms are yellow on the underside, while winter forms are a light cocoa brown. Both forms show a diagonal rusty median patch, divided, on the hindwing. The upperside is deep orange-brown with black borders on both wings. It can be identified in flight by its distinctive orange color, pattern, and size. Flight is often fast, erratic, and usually low to the ground. Wingspan: 1.5–2.25 in.

Summer

Winter

When and Where: Widespread and usually abundant year-round. It can be expected almost anywhere but especially at roadside wildflowers and in gardens. Larval foodplants consist of a variety of legumes, including *Cassia* species and clover.

Similar Species: Boisduval's Yellow (*page 59*) is most alike but is paler, and the rusty hindwing patch is curved. Mexican Yellow (*page 60*) is also similar but larger and paler. The Tailed Orange winter form (*page 62*) is similar but has a more prominently angled hindwing.

Remarks: Its name probably refers to the broken median line that resembles two closed eyes (or one closed, one open), accentuated by the two small outer spots that may be seen as a nose.

Sulphurs—Subfamily Coliadinae

Dainty Sulphur *Nathalis iole*

The smallest of the sulphurs, its two-toned pattern is usually evident even at a distance. It is seasonally dimorphic: summer forms are yellowish with a faint blackish wash on the hindwing; winter forms have a solid-gray hindwing. Both forms have a golden-yellow forewing with a broad dusky wingtip and a pair of black submarginal spots. The upperside has a broad black wingtip and a dark spot near the trailing edge of the forewing. Flight is usually fast and low to the ground. Wingspan: .75–1.25 in.

When and Where: Widespread and common (sometimes abundant) year-round. It prefers open areas, including roadways and flats with little vegetation. Larval foodplants consist of a wide variety of composites, including daisies, rabbitbrush, ragweed, and thistles.

Similar Species: No other little sulphur has a two-toned underside and two black forewing spots. The upperside of the female Barred Yellow (*page 57*) is somewhat alike, but it has dark hindwing margins.

Remarks: Once known as "Dwarf Yellow," due to its small size, it is often the only active butterfly species on chilly mornings.

Mimic-Whites—Subfamily Dismorphiinae

Mimic-Whites are small, tropical species with a hindwing that is noticeably larger than the forewing. Sexually dimorphic, they are represented by a single species in the LRGV.

Costa-spotted Mimic-White *Enantia albania*

LRGV specialty. Sexually dimorphic, but the hindwing is noticeably larger than the forewing on both sexes. Males are yellow with a large scaleless patch on the underside of the hindwing; females have a white hindwing and a yellow forewing with a black margin and squared apex. The upperside is similar. Wingspan: .75–1.25 in.

When and Where: Accidental, with historical records only in September. It does occur in nearby Mexico, so additional sightings are possible. Larval foodplants are unknown.

Similar Species: It is similar in size to Little Yellow (*page 63*) and **Mimosa Yellow** (*page 64*), but they lack the larger hindwing.

Remarks: Flight is slow and fluttering.

Gossamer-wing Butterflies— Family Lycaenidae

This family includes small to medium-sized butterflies that are often brightly colored with iridescent blues, reds, and oranges. Most have an eyespot near the lower angle of the hindwing. Adults usually rest with their wings closed, and their flight is swift and darting, oftentimes difficult to follow.

Hairstreaks—Subfamily Theclinae

Hairstreaks are small to medium-sized butterflies that range in color from dull browns and grays to iridescent blues and greens. Most species have thin tails that can be quite long. They have a habit of rubbing their hindwings back and forth while feeding, a behavior believed to draw a predator's attention to the butterfly's less vulnerable rear end, rather than its head.

Strophius Hairstreak *Allosmaitia strophius*

LRGV specialty. The underside is gray-brown with jagged black and white postmedian lines on the hindwing, along with a red-edged black tailspot. The forewing has a short, dark, smudged postmedian line. The upperside is darker brown. The male has bright blue patches on the hindwing and inner margin of the forewing. Wingspan: 1–1.25 in.

When and Where: Accidental, in October and November. There are historical records only. Since this species does occur in nearby Mexico, additional sightings are possible. Larval foodplants include Barbados-cherry.

Similar Species: No other gray-brown hairstreak has an obvious, smudged postmedian line on the underside of the forewing.

Remarks: Some authors refer to this species as "Blue-metal Hairstreak," and its earlier specific scientific name was "*pion*."

Hairstreaks—Subfamily Theclinae

Great Purple Hairstreak *Atlides halesus*

Large for a hairstreak, the Great Purple is a gorgeous creature. The underside is an overall purplish-gray with metallic red basal spots and a bright red abdomen. It has one or two long, often twisted, threadlike tails. The upperside is a brilliant iridescent blue on males, somewhat duller on females. Both have broad dark margins. Wingspan: 1.25–2 in.

When and Where: Widespread but uncommon year-round. It feeds on a variety of flowers, so it can be expected in gardens as well as on flowering plants along roadsides. Most sightings are of solitary individuals, but it is occasionally found in numbers. Larval foodplants are limited to mistletoes.

Similar Species: No other butterfly found regularly in the LRGV could possibly be confused with this large, beautiful hairstreak.

Remarks: One would think that this outstanding butterfly is tropical in origin, but it occurs throughout the southern United States, from coast to coast. It occasionally strays north to the Northwest, upper Midwest, and Northeast.

Hairstreaks—Subfamily Theclinae

Gold-bordered Hairstreak   *Rekoa palegon*

LRGV specialty. The underside is gray with irregular bands of reddish streaks on the hindwing, squares on the forewing, and wide orange-brown margins. The upperside is bright blue on males and gray-blue to pale brown on females. Wingspan: 1–1.25 in.

When and Where: Accidental, with historical records in November. It occurs in nearby Mexico, so additional sightings are possible. Larval foodplants include asters and verbena in Mexico.

Similar Species: No other LRGV hairstreak is likely to be confused with a fresh Gold-bordered.

Remarks: Opler states that this species frequents "disturbed areas in a wide variety of tropical environments."

Hairstreaks—Subfamily Theclinae

Marius Hairstreak *Rekoa marius*

LRGV specialty. The underside is gray-brown with parallel black and white dashed median lines on the hindwing and the forewing, a faint submarginal band of gray, and a pair of red-capped black tailspots. The upperside is deep blue on males and brownish with a pale trailing area on the female's hindwing. Wingspan: 1–1.5 in.

When and Where: Accidental, from September to December. It occurs in nearby Mexico, so additional LRGV sightings are possible. Larval foodplants include legumes.

Similar Species: Gray Hairstreak (*page 81*) is somewhat alike on the underside but has a narrow all-black submarginal line.

Remarks: There are five species of *Rekoa* hairstreaks in northeast Mexico; all are difficult to separate in the field.

Black Hairstreak *Ocaria ocrisia*

LRGV specialty. A blackish-brown hairstreak with a pair of broken whitish lines on the hindwing and with median and marginal lines on the forewing. The upperside is black with iridescent blue on males and brown with a blue hindwing margin on females. Wingspan: .75–1 in.

When and Where: Accidental, in January and November. Although it is uncommon in nearby Mexico, additional sightings are possible. Larval foodplants are unknown.

Similar Species: No other hairstreak has such a dark upperside.

Remarks: The first U.S. record of this species occurred in the aftermath of Hurricane Beulah in 1968.

Hairstreaks—Subfamily Theclinae

Telea Hairstreak *Chlorostrymon telea*

The underside is chartreuse with a postmedian line on the hindwing that forms a W on the inner margin of a large reddish-brown patch near the tail. The upperside is reddish-purple on males and brown with blue hindwing patches on females. Wingspan: .75 in.

When and Where: Accidental, with a lone historical sighting in June. A resident of south Florida, the larvae feed on the foliage of West Indies mahogany.

Similar Species: Silver-banded Hairstreak (*page 74*) is somewhat alike but has a much wider postmedian band on the hindwing and a more extensive brown marginal patch.

Remarks: Scott refers to this little hairstreak as "Verde Azul."

Silver-banded Hairstreak *Chlorostrymon simaethis*

LRGV specialty. This beautiful little hairstreak is mostly green on the underside with a straight, broad, silvery band (edged with red) that crosses both wings, and a broad brownish patch on the hindwing margin. The dark tails are hardly noticeable. The upperside is iridescent purple on males but duller on females. Wingspan: .75–1.25 in.

When and Where: Uncommon and local on or near balloonvines year-round. Balloonvine, its larval foodplant, grows on shrubs and fences throughout the eastern half of the LRGV.

Similar Species: **Clench's** (*page 76*), **Goodson's** (*page 77*), and **Tropical** (*page 78*) **greenstreaks** also have green undersides, but none has a broad hindwing patch. The **Xami Hairstreak** (*page 79*) is also similar but is brownish-green with a "spiked" hindwing band. Telea Hairstreak (*page 73*) is similar and has a broad hindwing patch, but it lacks the silvery band on the underside.

Remarks: Truly one of the Valley's most appealing butterflies. Balloonvine is easily identified by its one-inch-wide inflated seed pods.

Hairstreaks—Subfamily Theclinae

Oak Hairstreak *Satyrium favonius*

The underside is gray-brown with wavy white and brown postmedian lines that form a W near the inner margin. A submarginal line of red patches terminates at a square, blue-gray tail patch. The forewing has broken postmedian and submarginal lines. The upperside is brown with pale-orange tailspots. Wingspan: 1.25–1.5 in.

When and Where: Accidental, in April and May. It is common in northeastern Texas, so additional sightings are possible. Larval food-plants include oaks.

Similar Species: Gray Hairstreak (*page 81*) is most alike but is gray and lacks the square blue-gray tail patch.

Remarks: Some authors refer to the subspecies (*ontario*) that occurs north and west of Florida as "Northern Oak Hairstreaks" and the Florida subspecies (*favonius*) as "Southern Oak Hairstreaks."

Hairstreaks—Subfamily Theclinae

Clench's Greenstreak *Cyanophrys miserabilis*

LRGV specialty. The underside is yellow-green with a series of faint white median lines, a short reddish submarginal line, dual maroon and black tailspots, and a very short tail. The upperside is iridescent blue with brown margins on males and brown with a grayish base on females. The head is brown. Wingspan: .75–1.25 in.

When and Where: Rare and local, with records from April to December. Until recent years, it was regularly found near ratamas, its larval foodplant, but it has since disappeared. Because it is fairly common in nearby Mexico, additional sightings are possible.

Similar Species: **Goodson's** (*page 77*) and **Tropical** (*page 78*) **greenstreaks** are very similar, but Goodson's is tailless and Tropical lacks the dual maroon and black tailspots.

Remarks: Because it was once resident in the LRGV, it is likely to recolonize. Scott refers to this species as "Sad Green Hairstreak."

Goodson's Greenstreak *Cyanophrys goodsoni*

LRGV specialty. The underside of this tailless greenstreak is green with scattered reddish markings, maroon spots at the anal angle, and dark hindwing edges. The head is green. The upperside is blue and gray, darker near the wingtips. Wingspan: .75–1.25 in.

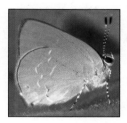

When and Where: Accidental, from May to December. Fairly common in nearby Mexico, so additional sightings are possible. Its larval foodplant is pigeon-berry, a common undergrowth plant of woodland areas.

Similar Species: **Clench's** (*page 76*) and **Tropical** (*page 78*) **greenstreaks** are very similar, but both have a short tail.

Remarks: Bordelon and Knudson point out that this species was "formerly fairly common," but that its foodplants have "been extirpated in many areas by the spread of introduced grasses."

Hairstreaks—Subfamily Theclinae

Tropical Greenstreak *Cyanophrys herodotus*

LRGV specialty. The underside is green with a short broken median line of white and reddish streaks, a small orange submarginal spot, a black tailspot, and short tails. The upperside is lavender-blue. The front of the head is green. Wingspan: .75–1.25 in.

When and Where: Accidental, in May, June, and October. Fairly common in nearby Mexico, so additional sightings are possible. Larval foodplants include various verbenas, such as lantanas, as well as pepper-tree.

Similar Species: **Clench's** (*page 76*) and **Goodson's** (*page 77*) **greenstreaks** are similar. Clench's has a marginal spot on the hindwing and a brown head. Goodson's Greenstreak is tailless.

Remarks: Scott refers to this species as "Tropical Green Hairstreak."

Hairstreaks—Subfamily Theclinae

Xami Hairstreak   *Callophrys xami*

LRGV specialty. A small olive-brown hairstreak (sometimes quite green) with a narrow white hindwing band (red on the inner edge) that curves outward toward brown and gray spots near the rather long tails. There are white-edged brown squares in front of the brown and gray tailspots. The upperside is golden-brown, darker on the outer portions. Flight, unlike most hairstreaks, is usually slow and near the ground. Wingspan: .75–1.25 in.

When and Where: Fairly common but local year-round. It occurs only in arid cactus-scrub sites with plenty of stonecrop and echeveria, its larval foodplants. The best place to find this butterfly is along Old Port Isabel Road, off FM 511.

Similar Species: In the LRGV, it can only be confused with a worn **Silver-banded Hairstreak** (*page 74*), which is green rather than brownish-green and has a straight hindwing band.

Remarks: This hairstreak is sometimes known as "Succulent Hairstreak," due to the succulent larval foodplants it uses.

Aquamarine Hairstreak *Oenomaus ortygnus*

LRGV specialty. The underside of this medium-sized hairstreak is gray with several black spots, including two median spots, and a wide aquamarine band (divided by a gray line) on the trailing edge of the hindwing. The upperside is iridescent greenish-blue on males and pale blue on females. The legs are banded black-and-white, and the tip of the antenna club is orange. Wingspan: 1.25–1.5 in.

When and Where: Accidental, in November and December. Since it occurs regularly in nearby Mexico, additional sightings are possible. There are no known larval foodplants in the U.S.

Similar Species: No other LRGV butterfly has similar features.

Remarks: The most recent record was of one photographed by Jan Dauphin at the NABA garden in November 2003.

Hairstreaks—Subfamily Theclinae

Gray Hairstreak *Strymon melinus*

This hairstreak can vary from slate-gray to almost white. It has two lines across the underside of each wing. The inner line is composed of several bars marked with white, black, and red (inner side); the submarginal line is black. Two red-capped, black tailspots are present near the pair of tails. The upperside is largely unmarked except for a pair of large, orange-capped, black tailspots. Wingspan: 1–1.5 in.

When and Where: Widespread and common year-round. It frequents flowering plants of all sizes and kinds throughout the LRGV. Larval foodplants span a wide diversity of species.

Similar Species: There are several somewhat similar but slightly smaller hairstreaks (*pages 82–91*) with whitish to gray or brownish tones, but Gray Hairstreak is the only one with a pair of lines on the underside without additional spots, bars, or mottling.

Remarks: Because the caterpillars can feed on a great variety of plants, Gray Hairstreak is considered the most widespread of North American butterflies.

Hairstreaks—Subfamily Theclinae

Red-crescent Scrub-Hairstreak *Strymon rufofusca*

LRGV specialty. A small, gray-brown hairstreak with an uneven post-median line of tiny red and white crescents and two orange-capped black tailspots separated by a gray square. The upperside is brown with dark veins and has a red-capped black tailspot. The legs are pale, and the antennae club is tipped in orange. Wingspan: .75–1.25 in.

When and Where: Occasional, from March to January. It frequents flowering plants throughout the region. Larval foodplants include various mallows.

Similar Species: Red-lined Scrub-Hairstreak (*page 83*) is most alike but is paler, usually larger, and has a submarginal band of white-edged brown crescents. Gray Hairstreak (*page 81*) is also similar but considerably larger and has two lines on the hindwing.

Remarks: Some authors refer to this species as "Reddish Hairstreak," since individuals may have a reddish cast.

Hairstreaks—Subfamily Theclinae

Red-lined Scrub-Hairstreak *Strymon bebrycia*

The underside is gray to tan with a single broken postmedian line of red and white dashes, a submarginal band of white-edged brown crescents, and two red-capped black tailspots. Wingspan: 1–1.25 in.

When and Where: Occasional, from October to November. Its larval foodplant is balloonvine, which is common in various locations throughout the eastern half of the LRGV.

Similar Species: Gray Hairstreak (*page 81*) is most alike but has two lines on the underside of the hindwing. **Red-crescent Scrub-Hairstreak** (*page 82*) is also similar, but it is smaller, gray-brown to reddish, and lacks the submarginal band of white-edged brown crescents.

Remarks: Scott refers to this species as "Balloon-vine Hairstreak," because of its larval foodplant. There are also records of this species in west Texas and Arizona.

Yojoa Scrub-Hairstreak *Strymon yojoa*

LRGV specialty. The underside is gray with considerable dark mottling, a red, black, and white postmedian line, and a slightly darker, gray-white submarginal band on the hindwing. The forewing has a short white center bar (post-basal stripe). The upperside is dark gray-brown with two large, white-edged, blackish hindwing spots. Wingspan: .75–1.25 in.

When and Where: Occasional, in April and from October to January. It is somewhat regular at flowering shrubs and is most likely to be found at Santa Ana NWR. Larval foodplants include tickclover and hibiscus.

Similar Species: Lacey's Scrub-Hairstreak (*page 86*) is most alike but has more distinct, jagged, white, black, and red postmedian lines and lacks the grayish submarginal and marginal bands. **White Scrub-Hairstreak** (*page 85*) is two-toned and lacks the red, black, and white postmedian line on the hindwing.

Remarks: Scott called this species "White-stripe Hairstreak," for the white forewing bar.

White Scrub-Hairstreak *Strymon albata*

LRGV specialty. The underside is noticeably two-toned. The basal half is gray-brown, and the outer half is white with numerous pale-brown submarginal crescents. There is a white patch at the anal margin and three faint, orange-capped, black tailspots. The upperside is white with brownish patches. The legs are banded black-and-white, and the tip of the black antennae club is orange. Wingspan: 1.25–1.5 in.

When and Where: Rare, with records in April and from June to December. Most sightings occur in fall at flowering shrubs. Larval foodplants may be limited to Indianmallow.

Similar Species: **Yojoa Scrub-Hairstreak** (*page 84*) is most alike but lacks the contrasting two-toned, white-and-brown pattern on the underside.

Remarks: The outer half of the hindwing can be snow-white.

Lacey's Scrub-Hairstreak *Strymon alea*

Another small, gray-brown hairstreak, the underside has red, black, and white postmedian lines (darker in winter) that are uneven but continuous and terminate in a forward sweep on the inner margin of the hindwing. It has considerable mottling above and below the postmedian line, a submarginal band of white-edged brown spots, and two large, orange-capped, black tailspots. The upperside is blackish-brown with a two white-edged tailspots. Wingspan: .75–1.25 in.

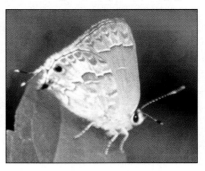

When and Where: Uncommon and local at scattered sites, in April and from October to December. It never seems to stray far from its larval foodplant, myrtlecroton, a relatively common shrub in drier areas of Santa Ana NWR and elsewhere.

Similar Species: Yojoa Scrub-Hairstreak (*page 84*) is most alike, but the postmedian line is straighter and stronger. Red-lined Scrub-Hairstreak (*page 83*) is also alike but lacks the abundant hindwing mottling above and below the postmedian line. Mallow Scrub-Hairstreak (*page 87*) is also similar but can readily be separated by its two spots near the leading edge of the hindwing.

Remarks: The Texas range of this species coincides with that of its larval foodplant along the Rio Grande and northward into the southern portion of the Hill Country.

Hairstreaks—Subfamily Theclinae

Mallow Scrub-Hairstreak *Strymon istapa*

This small, gray-brown hairstreak is well marked on the underside with two reddish-black spots along the leading edge of the hindwing, broken white, black, and red postmedian lines, numerous white-capped, brown submarginal spots, and two orange-capped, black tailspots, the top one noticeably larger. The upperside is brownish on males and blue-gray on females; both have two or three blackish marginal spots near the tail. Tails may become worn and hardly noticeable. Wingspan: .75–1.25 in.

When and Where: Widespread and common year-round. It frequents flowering plants throughout the area and can almost always be found with some searching. Larval foodplants consist of various mallows.

Similar Species: Red-lined (*page 83*), **Red-crescent** (*page 82*), and Lacey's (*page 86*) scrub-hairstreaks are similar, but they all lack the two spots along the leading edge of the hindwing. Ceraunus Blue (*page 102*) is also similar but is tailless.

Remarks: This hairstreak was formerly known as "Common Hairstreak" and "Columella Hairstreak" (*S. columella*).

Tailless Scrub-Hairstreak *Strymon cestri*

LRGV specialty. This butterfly's underside is mottled white, gray, and black, and it is tailless. The hindwing has a postmedian band of brown spots, a lone brown spot at the center of the leading edge, and a black submarginal spot. The forewing is brownish-gray with a median band of tiny crescents and broad, gray dual submarginal bands. The upperside is brown on males, with blue showing on females. Both have three whitish-capped black tailspots. Wingspan: .75–1.25 in.

When and Where: Accidental, in March. It occurs in nearby Mexico, so additional sightings are possible. Larval foodplants are unknown.

Similar Species: Lantana Scrub-Hairstreak (*page 89*) is most alike. It, too, lacks a tail, but it is mostly brown with a prominent brown spot near the leading edge of the hindwing underside.

Remarks: Scott refers to this species as "Spotted Hairstreak."

Hairstreaks—Subfamily Theclinae

Lantana Scrub-Hairstreak *Strymon bazochii*

LRGV specialty. This small, tailless hairstreak is mostly gray-brown on the underside with a large brown spot near the leading edge of the hindwing, a pale diagonal hindwing bar, and a pale apical region on the forewing. The upperside is dark gray-brown with blue on the trailing portion of the hindwing. The fringes are white. Wingspan: .75–1 in.

When and Where: Occasional much of the year, with sightings from January to March, in May, and from October to December. Most likely at flowering plants in shaded sites, such as at Santa Ana NWR. Larval foodplants include lantana, lippia, and frog-fruit.

Similar Species: The similar **Tailless Scrub-Hairstreak** (*page 88*) is mottled white, gray, and black with a postmedian band of brown spots.

Remarks: This little butterfly has been introduced to Hawaii to control an introduced invasive shrub, *Lantana camera*.

Hairstreaks—Subfamily Theclinae

Ruddy Hairstreak *Electrostrymon sangala*

LRGV specialty. The underside is pale brown with rather straight, red and white postmedian lines and two red-capped, black tailspots, one large and one very small, on the hindwing. The upperside is golden-orange with brown veins and brown on the leading portion of the forewing on males. Females are pale brown with a faint black tailspot. Wingspan: .75–1 in.

When and Where: Accidental, in April and from October to December. It is present in small numbers in nearby Mexico, so additional sightings are possible. Larval foodplants include coralbean.

Similar Species: No other LRGV hairstreak has such drab colors on the underside with such a contrasting upperside. **Muted Hairstreak** (*page 91*) is similar on the underside but is slightly larger. The upperside is dark brown. The rare Mountain Groundstreak (*page 93*) is also similar on the underside but has faint orange submarginal crescents. Males are dark brown on the upperside; females lack the faint black tailspot.

Remarks: One earlier specific scientific name of this hairstreak was "*endymion*."

Hairstreaks—Subfamily Theclinae

Muted Hairstreak *Electrostrymon canus*

LRGV specialty. The underside of the hindwing is brown, with red and white postmedian lines that form a W near the inner margin, submarginal dark lines edged with white, two black tailspots, one large and one smaller, edged with pale orange, and a blue-gray tail patch that extends outward. The upperside is dark brown with a blackish apical area. Wingspan: 1–1.25 in.

When and Where: Accidental, dates unknown. Since it does occur in nearby Mexico, additional sightings are possible. Larval foodplants include foliage of mangos.

Similar Species: **Ruddy Hairstreak** (*page 90*) is very similar but is slightly smaller. The males are golden-orange on the upperside.

Remarks: This species is easily confused with Ruddy Hairstreak; females are impossible to separate in the field.

Dusky-blue Groundstreak *Calycopis isobeon*

The underside is a warm brown with red and white postmedian bands on the hindwing that form a W in front of two red-capped black tailspots, divided by a large bluish square. The upperside is brown with a large bluish patch on the inner margin of the hindwing that is often evident in flight. Wingspan: .75–1 in.

When and Where: Widespread and common year-round. It frequents flowering shrubs but also occurs on or near the ground in grasses and debris. It has a tendency to seek shady areas, including the protected sides of buildings, at midday. Rotting leaves are eaten by the caterpillars.

Similar Species: Although it can look like several other small, brown, worn hairstreaks, none of the other LRGV hairstreaks have the large bluish hindwing patch and double red-capped, black tailspots.

Remarks: This species has multiple broods and numbers can be abundant following emergence. The closely related Red-banded Hairstreak does not reach south Texas.

Mountain Groundstreak *Ziegleria guzanta*

The underside of the hindwing is yellowish-brown with a jagged white postmedian line, an orange-capped, dark-brown tailspot just above a square gray patch, and a series of orange (often faint) submarginal crescents. The forewing has a reddish median line and faint reddish lines running the length of the wing. The upperside is generally unmarked; males are darker brown than females. Wingspan: .75–1 in.

When and Where: Accidental, a single record from January 2004. Since this species occurs in nearby Mexico, additional sightings are possible. Larval foodplants are unknown.

Similar Species: **Ruddy Hairstreak** (*page 90*) is most alike but lacks the orange submarginal crescents on the underside of the hindwing. Males are golden-orange on the upperside; females have a faint black tailspot.

Remarks: This 2004 record is one of several new LRGV records documented by Dave Hanson. There are also three records from west Texas. Some authors place this species in the genus *Kisutam*.

Red-spotted Hairstreak *Tmolus echion*

LRGV specialty. The underside is gray-brown with a crooked red post-median line, several black-edged, red median spots, and two orange-capped, black tailspots. The upperside is brownish with an iridescent blue basal area extending onto the wings on males. Females are bluish-gray on the upperside. Wingspan: 1–1.25 in.

When and Where: Accidental, with historical records only in May. Since it is fairly common in nearby Mexico, additional sightings are possible. Larval foodplants include lantana.

Similar Species: **Clytie Ministreak** (*page 96*) is most alike but is smaller and lacks the iridescent blue upperside. The red spots on the hind-wing underside lack black edges.

Remarks: This species was once introduced to Hawaii to control spreading lantana.

Pearly-gray Hairstreak *Siderus tephraeus*

LRGV specialty. The underside is pearly-gray with two postmedian lines of white streaks, a submarginal line of white-edged brownish spots, and a small, orange-capped, black tailspot. The upperside is iridescent blue on males and dull brown on females, both with black wingtips. Wingspan: 1–1.25 in.

When and Where: Accidental, from September to December. Since it's fairly common in nearby Mexico, additional sightings are possible. Larval foodplants are unknown in the United States.

Similar Species: No other hairstreak has such pearly-gray underparts and bright-blue upperparts.

Remarks: Many authors refer to this species as "Tephraeus Hairstreak," after its specific scientific name.

Clytie Ministreak *Ministrymon clytie*

LRGV specialty. The underside is marked with numerous orange-red rectangles that form double lines across the gray hindwings, white submarginal mottling on both wings, and two orange-capped, black tailspots. Darker in winter. The upperside includes a brown forewing and a gray hindwing on males; it is mostly brown on females. Both have two small, black tailspots. Wingspan: .75–1 in.

Summer

Winter

When and Where: Common but local year-round. It can be abundant at certain locations, such as Laguna Atascosa NWR, where hundreds can sometimes be found in summer. Larval foodplants consist of legumes, including mesquites.

Similar Species: Red-lined (*page 83*), **Red-crescent** (*page 82*), and Lacey's (*page 86*) scrub-hairstreaks and **Gray Ministreak** (*page 97*) are similar but lack the double line of red rectangles across the hindwings. The larger **Red-spotted Hairstreak** (*page 94*) has a similar pattern of red spots on the hindwing underside, but they are black-edged. Its upperside is iridescent blue.

Remarks: This little hairstreak commonly perches on the underside of leaves.

Hairstreaks—Subfamily Theclinae

Gray Ministreak *Ministrymon azia*

LRGV specialty. A tiny gray hairstreak with somewhat jagged red and white postmedian lines, faint whitish submarginal spots, a very narrow red marginal line, and two red-capped, black tailspots on the hindwing. The upperside is uniformly dark brown. Wingspan: .5–.75 in.

When and Where: Occasional, from March to October. Because of its tiny size and solitary habit, it may be more common than reported. Larval foodplants include soft-leaf mimosa.

Similar Species: No other hairstreak is so small and so finely marked.

Remarks: Some authors refer to this species as "Azia Ministreak," after its specific scientific name.

Blues—Subfamily Polyommatinae

Blues are tiny to small butterflies that are usually sexually dimorphic; the upperside of males is typically bright, showy blue, while that of females is dull-brown to gray. They usually occur near their larval foodplants and rarely fly long distances. Flight is swift, often low and erratic, and may be difficult to follow.

Western Pygmy-Blue *Brephidium exile*

Considered the world's smallest butterfly, the Western Pygmy-Blue is a lovely creature that is readily identified by its tiny size. The underside of the forewing is golden-brown, and the hindwing is gray with a row of black submarginal spots. The upperside is mostly brown with a bluish base. Wingspan: .5–.75 in.

When and Where: Common but local year-round. Most abundant in open fields and near wetlands where its larval foodplants grow. They include a variety of goosefoot species, such as pickleweed and saltbushes.

Similar Species: No other tiny butterfly has the gray-and-golden-brown wing pattern on the underside.

Remarks: It can be overlooked because of its tiny size, but it will usually allow close-up observations and photographs if you approach slowly and do not allow your shadow to frighten it off.

Blues—Subfamily Polyommatinae

Cassius Blue *Leptotes cassius*

The underside is white with a multitude of jagged gray-brown stripes and circles. A series of submarginal eyespots—dark-centered white circles—is present on the forewing and upper hindwing. The lower portion of the hindwing has a pair of large, pale-orange-edged, black tailspots. The upperside is violet on males and white with brownish streaks and margins on females. Wingspan: .75–1 in.

When and Where: Widespread but occasional year-round. Most sightings are in the eastern portion of the LRGV, usually on flowering plants. Larval foodplants include several legumes.

Similar Species: The slightly larger Marine Blue (*page 100*) is gray-brown overall on the underside, with white marks that form closed oblong rings on the hindwing.

Remarks: Cassius Blue has a divided range, with one population in south Texas and Mexico and the other in Florida. It occasionally wanders northward to Colorado and Kansas.

Blues—Subfamily Polyommatinae

Marine Blue *Leptotes marina*

The underside has a multitude of gray oblong circles with purplish (males) or tan (females) centers, margins lined with dark crescents capped with gray, and a pair of orange-capped, black tailspots. The upperside is lavender-blue in males and brown in females; both have a pair of black tailspots. Wingspan: .75–1.25 in.

When and Where: Widespread but uncommon year-round. Populations can vary greatly. In spite of its name, it is more common in the drier western parts of the Valley than closer to the coast. Larval foodplants are limited to legumes, such as acacias, beans, daleas, and mesquites.

Similar Species: Cassius Blue (*page 99*) is very similar but is more extensively white on the underside and lacks the oblong rings on the hindwing.

Remarks: This blue is known for its extensive northward movements in fall, sometimes flying (probably assisted by wind currents) more than 500 miles.

Blues—Subfamily Polyommatinae

Cyna Blue *Zizula cyna*

The Cyna Blue is tiny and gray with long, slender forewings and short, rounded hindwings. The underside of the hindwing has a postmedian line of black spots and a similar basal line, with two black spots near the leading edge. The forewing has a line of black postmedian spots. The upperside is lavender-gray, with brownish-gray near the margins. Flight is low and weak. Wingspan: .5–.75 in.

When and Where: Rare, with records from March to January. Most sightings are from low-growing flowering shrubs in gardens. Larval foodplants are unknown.

Similar Species: No other blue with an all-gray underside is so small.

Remarks: Often known as "Tiny Blue," it wanders widely, in spite of its size.

Blues—Subfamily Polyommatinae

Ceraunus Blue *Hemiargus ceraunus*

The gray-brown underside has two black spots on the leading edge of the hindwing, a row of pale submarginal crescents, and one or two large black eyespots. The upperside is lavender-blue on males and pale blue on females. The male's lavender-blue color is often evident in flight. Wingspan: .75–1 in.

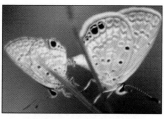

When and Where: Widespread and common year-round. Most numerous near the coast. It prefers to feed on low-growing flowering plants. Larval foodplants include several legumes, such as acacias, mesquites, and sennas.

Similar Species: Reakirt's Blue (*page 103*) is most alike but has black postmedian spots on the forewing. Ceraunus Blue also resembles Mallow Scrub-Hairstreak (*page 87*), but Ceraunus Blue lacks a tail.

Remarks: An earlier name of this blue was "Antillean Blue," due to its affinity for the warm southeastern lowlands.

Blues—Subfamily Polyommatinae

Reakirt's Blue *Hemiargus isola*

This little grayish butterfly is well marked on the underside of the forewing with a row of five large, black postmedian spots, ringed in white, and a lone dark or black bar. It also has a scattering of black spots and bars on the hindwing and numerous dark crescents along the margins. The upperside is deep blue in males and brownish-blue in females. Both have one large and often two additional small black tailspots. Wingspan: .75–1.25 in.

When and Where: Widespread and fairly common year-round. It is most likely to be found at weedy sites with wildflowers. Larval food-plants include various legumes, such as acacias, daleas, mesquites, and mimosas.

Similar Species: No other blue has a row of large black postmedian spots and a dark or black bar on the underside of the forewing.

Remarks: Reakirt's Blues are usually commonplace in the LRGV, but there are periods when they are difficult to find. Reakirt's Blue tends to be a loner and is sometimes known as "Solitary Blue."

Blues—Subfamily Polyommatinae

Eastern Tailed-Blue *Everes comyntas*

The only tailed blue in the LRGV, the underside of the hindwing is white to gray with a postmedian row of short dark lines, a series of gray marginal crescents, and two orange-capped, black tailspots. The upperside is marine blue on males and brown on females, both with tailspots. Like hairstreaks, it has a habit of rubbing its hindwings together when feeding. Wingspan: .75–1 in.

When and Where: Rare and local, with records from July and August. This strange little blue is most likely to be seen near the coast. Larval foodplants consist of several members of the pea family, including clovers, locoweeds, lupines, peas, and vetches.

Similar Species: Mallow Scrub-Hairstreak (*page 87*) is most alike but is brown with two black spots on the leading edge of the hindwing underside.

Remarks: Eastern Tailed-Blues range across eastern North America and south into Mexico.

Metalmarks—Family Riodinidae

Metalmarks are small to medium-sized butterflies, and most have obvious bands of shiny, metallic-looking scales, especially on the underside. The front legs of males are reduced in size and are not used for walking. Adults normally rest and feed with their wings spread.

Fatal Metalmark *Calephelis nemesis*

The upperside is brownish to dark gray-brown with a wide, darker brown median band across both wings, which are paler toward the margins. The silvery postmedian line, though often weak, is fairly straight. Males have pointed forewings. The underside is yellow-orange with thin metallic postmedian lines and broken blue submarginal lines. Wingspan: .75–1 in.

When and Where: Widespread and common year-round, most numerous from May to December. The Fatal Metalmark is most likely to be found near its larval foodplants, virgin's-bower and seep-willow.

Similar Species: Rounded (*page 106*) and Rawson's (*page 107*) metalmarks are most alike. Rounded Metalmark has a silvery postmedian line that bulges outward in the center of the forewing. Rawson's Metalmark is extremely rare in the LRGV and lacks the obvious dark median band on the upperside.

Remarks: This is the most widespread and variable of the North American *Calephelis* metalmarks. The base color of this species can vary considerably.

Metalmarks—Family Riodinidae

Rounded Metalmark *Calephelis perditalis*

The upperside is dark brown to reddish-brown with a moderately dark median band and a silvery postmedian line on the forewing that bulges outward at the center. Fresh individuals also exhibit reddish submarginal bands. Both sexes have slightly rounded forewings. The underside is orange-yellow with a broad, spotted, silver postmedian line and a solid silver submarginal line. Wingspan: .75–1 in.

When and Where: Widespread and common year-round. The Rounded is the metalmark most often found on flowering plants in the LRGV. Larval foodplants include various *Eupatorium* species, such as crucita, all marvelous butterfly magnets.

Similar Species: Fatal Metalmark (*page 105*) is most alike, but it never shows a bulging postmedian line on the forewing. The extremely rare Rawson's Metalmark (*page 107*) also lacks a bulging post-median line.

Remarks: Some earlier guides refer to this species as "Lost Metalmark," presumedly because it is often ignored among the better-known metalmarks.

Metalmarks—Family Riodinidae

Rawson's Metalmark *Calephelis rawsoni*

The upperside is brown, often reddish-brown on males and orange-brown on females. The postmedian band may be slightly darker but is often indistinct. The silvery postmedian line is fairly straight and continuous, and there are several black submarginal spots within open brown squares. The underside is orange-brown with silvery post-median and broken submarginal lines. Wingspan: .75–1 in.

When and Where: Extremely rare and local, with records from February to November. More likely in the western portion of the Valley. Larval foodplants include several *Eupatorium* species and frog-fruit.

Similar Species: Rounded Metalmark (*page 106*) is most alike but has a bulging postmedian line on the forewing. Fatal Metalmark (*page 105*) is also similar but its upperside postmedian band is wider and darker. Rawson's is also usually somewhat larger than either Rounded or Fatal metalmarks.

Remarks: Fatal or Rounded metalmarks are often misidentified as this butterfly. Many of the *Calephelis* metalmarks can be identified only by genitalia examination.

Red-bordered Metalmark *Caria ino*

LRGV specialty. Adults are sexually dimorphic, but both have long pointed wings with a curvy leading edge. The upperside of fresh males is black; females are dark brown. Both have relatively wide reddish margins. Both sexes have a rusty-orange underside, with conspicuous metallic-blue spots. Wingspan: .75–1 in.

When and Where: Widespread and often common year-round. More common in the eastern portion of the LRGV, less numerous west of the Mission area. It feeds on a variety of flowering plants, often in gardens. Larval foodplants are limited to spiny hackberry.

Similar Species: A fresh male can hardly be confused with any other butterfly, but worn females could possibly be mistaken for a male **Curve-winged Metalmark** (*page 111*), but it lacks a wide reddish margin.

Remarks: When feeding, the Red-bordered often seems reluctant to fly.

Metalmarks—Family Riodinidae

Blue Metalmark *Lasaia sula*

LRGV specialty. Sexually dimorphic, males are bright blue on the upperside with scattered black lines, two black bars near the leading edge of the forewing, and dark wingtips. Females are gray-brown or blue-gray with similar features. The underside is patterned light-brown and white. Wingspan: .75–1 in.

When and Where: Uncommon and local year-round. It can be abundant at flowering shrubs, such as in the gardens at Sabal Palm Grove, Laguna Atascosa NWR, and Los Ebanos, especially in late summer and fall. It is seldom recorded west of Mission. Larval foodplants are unknown.

Similar Species: No other LRGV butterfly, especially males, can be mistaken for this gorgeous metalmark.

Remarks: Few butterflies so represent the tropics as this beautiful creature does.

Metalmarks—Family Riodinidae

Red-bordered Pixie *Melanis pixe*

LRGV specialty. A most unusual metalmark, it has coal-black wings with bright yellow wingtips, reddish-orange spots along the trailing edge of the hindwings, and a red spot at the base of each wing. The underside is similar. Flight is usually slow and fluttering. Wingspan: 1.5–2 in.

When and Where: Uncommon and local, in April, May, and from July to January. Populations exist throughout the eastern half of the LRGV, all at or near guamachil trees, its larval foodplant. Loners or a few individuals can also occasionally be found feeding in gardens.

Similar Species: No other butterfly could be confused with this beauty.

Remarks: The occurrence of Red-bordered Pixies appears to be on the rise, due to increased plantings of guamachil trees at gardens and elsewhere in the LRGV. When fresh Red-bordered Pixie chrysalises are found on the bark of guamachil trees, adults can usually be found among the foliage.

Curve-winged Metalmark *Emesis emesia*

LRGV specialty. Both sexes have a similar silhouette, with a curved leading edge of the forewing, and both have a white bar on the center of the leading edge. They are otherwise dimorphic. The upperside of males is mottled reddish-brown and black; females are orange-brown with numerous dark longitudinal streaks. The underside is pale brown to yellow with dark streaking. Wingspan: 1–1.25 in.

When and Where: Rare, in February and from May to December. One of the Valley's most-wanted species, it has been recorded most often in fall, usually feeding at flowering shrubs. Larval foodplants include bird-of-paradise and Mexican rushpea.

Similar Species: No other butterfly has the exaggerated, curved-wing pattern. **Red-bordered Metalmark** (*page 108*) has a slightly curved leading edge, but fresh individuals have wide reddish margins on both wings.

Remarks: Scott refers to this metalmark as "Big Curvy Wing."

Falcate Metalmark *Emesis tenedia*

LRGV specialty. The forewing is long and slightly falcate. Sexually dimorphic, males are mottled brown with a darker median bar on the forewing and several horizontal lines across the hindwing. Females are orange-brown with a similar pattern, except for a wider and paler median band on the forewing. The underside of males is orange-brown; females are yellow-brown, both with black markings. Wingspan: 1.25–1.5 in.

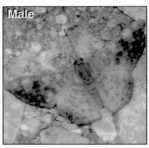 

When and Where: Accidental, a single record in October. The record was prior to 1980, making it an historical sighting. This species does occur in nearby Mexico, so additional sightings are possible. Larval foodplants include virgin's-bower.

Similar Species: The male **Curve-winged Metalmark** (*page 111*) is most alike, but the curved leading edge of its forewing and white bar are distinctive.

Remarks: Bordelon and Knudson state that a population of this species from Starr County apparently was "extirpated by cold winters in the mid-1990s."

Narrow-winged Metalmark *Apodemia multiplaga*

LRGV specialty. This metalmark has long, narrow, pointed forewings with a deep concave indentation on the outer margin below the wingtip. The upperside is blackish-brown with numerous bright white spots, a series of submarginal spots, and black-and-white checkered margins. The underside is pale brown or gray, yellowish toward the base, with a similar pattern. Wingspan: 1–1.25 in.

When and Where: Accidental, in October and November. It occurs in nearby Mexico, so additional sightings are possible. This species frequents open areas and often rests on the ground. Larval foodplants are unknown.

Similar Species: No other LRGV butterfly has the Narrow-winged's black-and-white pattern and concave wing margin.

Remarks: Scott refers to this species as "Pointed Metalmark," undoubtedly due to its pointed wingtips.

Metalmarks—Family Riodinidae

Walker's Metalmark *Apodemia walkeri*

LRGV specialty. The upperside is checkered with gray and brown and has a large dark to black patch on the leading edge of the forewing. It also has scattered dark-brown basal lines and spots on the forewing and similar dark-brown lines on the hindwing. Fresh individuals have a broad yellow-orange submarginal band on both wings. The underside is whitish with scattered brown markings and a pale-orange marginal band. Wingspan: .75–1 in.

When and Where: Rare, with records from May to August and October to December. Most often seen at gardens in the fall. Larval foodplants are unknown.

Similar Species: No other similar LRGV butterfly has a dark to black patch on the leading edge of the forewing.

Remarks: Scott refers to this species as "White Metalmark," because the underside is "mostly white."

Brushfooted Butterflies— Family Nymphalidae

All members of this family have reduced forelegs, although they have few other characteristics in common. The short legs are covered with hairs, especially on the males.

Snouts—Subfamily Libytheinae

The major feature of this subfamily is the extended palpi that provide the snout butterflies their name. They usually perch with wings folded but often bask spread-winged. The snout complex is rather complicated; some lepidopterists split this species into two species.

American Snout *Libytheana carinenta*

Its obvious "snout" (long palpi) readily identifies this unusual butterfly. The underside is mottled black, brown, and gray. The upperside is very different, with broad orange-brown stripes against a blackish background and a series of large white forewing spots. The wingtips are square. Wingspan: 1.5–2 in.

When and Where: Widespread and often the most abundant species year-round. It is especially common in areas of hackberry trees, its larval foodplant.

Similar Species: No other LRGV butterfly exhibits similar features.

Remarks: Snouts are famous for occasional mass movements when millions appear during late summer or fall and fly in enormous numbers.

Heliconians and Fritillaries—Subfamily Heliconiinae

Several species of these medium-sized to large butterflies are extremely colorful. Adults have elongated wings and long antennae. They often perch with wings spread. Flight is usually a slow flutter, but they can fly very fast when threatened. Many are distasteful or mimic distasteful species that predators shun. Fritillaries, members of this subfamily, are limited to only three species in the LRGV. They are more numerous and diverse in northern areas of the United States.

Gulf Fritillary *Agraulis vanillae*

The upperside of fresh individuals is bright orange-red with black-ringed white spots along the leading edge of the forewing and black-rimmed orange triangles on the trailing edge of the hindwing. The underside is even more colorful, with large, elongated silver patches against an orange-brown background. Wingspan: 2.5–3.75 in.

When and Where: Widespread and common year-round. It can be expected wherever flowering plants are present, whether along roadsides, in gardens, or at woodland edges. Larval foodplants are limited to passionflowers.

Similar Species: **Mexican Silverspot** (*page 118*), occasional only, is most alike, but the upperside basal area is dark brown. It lacks the black-ringed white spots. **Mexican Fritillary** (*page 128*) and Variegated Fritillary (*page 127*) are also similar, but neither has the black-ringed white spots or the silver-patched underside.

Remarks: Truly one of the Valley's most attractive butterflies, it also occurs throughout most of Texas and much of the South.

Heliconians and Fritillaries—Subfamily Heliconiinae

Mexican Silverspot *Dione moneta*

LRGV specialty. The upperside is orange with a dark-brown basal area and black-rimmed triangles along the trailing edge of the hindwing. The underside is dominated by silver patches against an orange background. Flight is usually swift and erratic. Wingspan: 2.75–3.25 in.

When and Where: Occasional, from April to January. Loners are most likely to be found in shaded areas or at woodland edges. Larval foodplants are limited to passionflowers.

Similar Species: The more common Gulf Fritillary (*page 116*), Variegated Fritillary (*page 127*), and **Mexican Fritillary** (*page 128*) are similar, but only Gulf Fritillary has a silver-patched underside. It lacks the dark basal area. A fresh Variegated Fritillary can have a slightly darker basal area, but both Variegated and Mexican fritillaries have a row of black submarginal hindwing spots, not present on the Mexican Silverspot.

Remarks: The Mexican Silverspot is not found every year, but it may be present more often than it's reported because of its similarity to the common Gulf Fritillary.

Banded Orange Heliconian *Dryadula phaetusa*

LRGV specialty. This longwing butterfly is bright orange with four dark-brown bands, three crossing the forewing and a wider median band crossing the hindwings. It also has a brown marginal band with an outer row of tiny pale spots. Males are brighter than females. The underside is similar but with a marginal row of pale crescents. Wingspan: 3–3.5 in.

When and Where: Accidental, recorded only in March, August, and November. Since this species is resident in nearby Mexico, additional sightings are possible. Larval foodplants are limited to passionflowers.

Similar Species: Only **Isabella's Heliconian** (*page 124*) is also orange and banded, but the outer half of its forewings are black with yellow bands.

Remarks: Adults are known to roost in small groups, "mostly under grass blades," according to Scott.

Julia Heliconian *Dryas iulia*

LRGV specialty. Another of the longwings with long, narrow wings, fresh Julias are bright orange above and below, especially males. The underside of females has a faint olive-brown wash. Flight is usually slow and fluttering. Wingspan: 3–3.75 in.

When and Where: Uncommon and local year-round. Julias are almost never found in open areas, instead preferring shaded places with native passionflowers, their larval foodplant. They do feed at gardens adjacent to woodlands, and northward wandering in late summer and fall is commonplace.

Similar Species: This relatively unmarked, orange, long-winged beauty would be difficult to mistake.

Remarks: Julia Heliconian, Zebra Heliconian, and several other closely related, long-winged butterflies can properly be referred to as "longwings," an earlier name.

Isabella's Heliconian *Eueides isabella*

LRGV specialty. This longwing has a contrasting pattern of orange-red and black on the hindwings, and broken yellow bands on the black outer half of the forewings. The underside is similar but paler. Wingspan: 2.75–3.5 in.

When and Where: Rare, with records throughout much of the year. Most sightings occur in fall, from October to December. Most likely to be found in gardens, its larval foodplants are limited to passionflowers.

Similar Species: **Banded Orange Heliconian** (*page 120*) is similar but lacks the black-and-yellow pattern on the outer half of the forewings.

Remarks: In spite of its tropical affinity, one strayed north as far as Austin, Texas in 1971.

Heliconians and Fritillaries—Subfamily Heliconiinae

Zebra Heliconian *Heliconius charithonia*

LRGV specialty. This longwing is zebra-striped, marked with broad pale to yellow bands that cross the black to brown wings. The underside is similar but has tiny red basal spots, sometimes also seen on the upperside. Wingspan: 2.75–3.75 in.

When and Where: Uncommon and local in woodland areas year-round. Most are found in shaded areas, but it also feeds on nearby flowering plants, including those in adjacent gardens. Larval foodplants include passionflowers.

Similar Species: No other butterfly has long, narrow wings with black and yellow stripes.

Remarks: Adults congregate at special roosts at night, and when feeding, they utilize trapline routes—a series of stops regularly visited. Zebras wander northward in late summer and fall, occasionally reaching north Texas and beyond. In some instances they colonize, and unless extirpated during a severe winter, a colony can last for several years.

Heliconians and Fritillaries—Subfamily Heliconiinae

LRGV specialty. This longwing is coal black with a broad crimson median band across the forewing and a yellow horizontal band near the leading edge of the hindwing. The underside is paler with whitish bands. Wingspan: 2.5–3 in.

When and Where: Rare, in January, June, August, and December. It is most likely to be found in woodland areas, such as Santa Ana NWR. Larval foodplants include passionflowers.

Similar Species: No other butterfly has a similar pattern.

Remarks: Some authors refer to this species as "Red-banded Longwing."

Heliconians and Fritillaries—Subfamily Heliconiinae

Variegated Fritillary *Euptoieta claudia*

More heavily marked than the other LRGV fritillaries, its upperside is orange-brown with a darker basal area and a black-rimmed pale-orange bar on the leading edge of the forewing. The trailing edge of the hindwing has a row of black-rimmed postmedian squares, with black spots in the centers, and a black submarginal line. The underside is pale orange-brown but crossed with a pale-gray postmedian band and a dark submarginal band on the hindwing. The forewing underside has a black-rimmed pale spot within an orange basal patch. Wingspan: 1.75–2.75 in.

When and Where: Widespread and common year-round. Most numerous in the western portion of the LRGV, especially in fields and more arid areas. It often rests on the ground. Larval foodplants include passionflowers, as well as a variety of other plants, including violets, flax, and plantain.

Similar Species: **Mexican Fritillary** (*page 128*) is most alike but has a relatively unmarked, pale-orange hindwing. Gulf Fritillary (*page 116*) and **Mexican Silverspot** (*page 118*) are also similar, but they lack the black-rimmed forewing bar and have silver patches on the underside.

Remarks: Variegated Fritillaries fly low over the ground with shallow wing beats, and when feeding, they often flutter over a flower, rather than alighting.

Mexican Fritillary *Euptoieta hegesia*

LRGV specialty. This fritillary is pale orange overall with two black-rimmed bars on the leading edge of the forewing. Both wings have a series of black spots inside a black submarginal line. The underside is generally unmarked except for a reddish-orange median band and apical area. Wingspan: 1.75–2.75 in.

When and Where: Uncommon and local most of the year, particularly in March and from July to December. This is a butterfly of shaded areas—especially in comparison with Variegated Fritillary—but it rarely visits gardens. Larval foodplants include damiana, passion-flowers, and morning glories.

Similar Species: It is most like Variegated Fritillary (*page 127*), but the upperside of the Mexican's hindwings have few markings. **Mexican Silverspot** (*page 118*) is also similar, but it has a dark-brown basal area and a silver-spotted underside.

Remarks: This Mexican species may be a periodic colonist in the LRGV. It wanders to the north and west in summer and fall.

Checkerspots, Patches, and Crescents—
Subfamily Nymphalinae

These medium-sized butterflies have rounded wings and show a variety of patterns and colors. Most have one or more crescent-shaped spots on the marginal area of the hindwing underside. They usually perch with wings spread.

Theona Checkerspot   *Thessalia theona*

The upperside is mostly black with orange and yellow bars and spots, including a postmedian band of long yellow bars and a series of orange submarginal spots. The broad margins are black with white flecks on the fringe. The underside has a median band of whitish oblong patches and a marginal band of whitish squares, divided by a band of black-edged rusty squares. Wingspan: 1–1.75 in.

When and Where: Widespread but uncommon, from March to January. This is a butterfly of more arid areas, where it utilizes ceniza and Indian paintbrush as larval foodplants. Adults feed on flowering plants along roadsides and in gardens. It can be abundant in areas dominated by ceniza, but it is rarely found in woodland sites.

Similar Species: The generally smaller Definite Patch (*page 131*) is most alike but lacks the postmedian band of long yellow bars.

Remarks: The pattern and color of this well-marked checkerspot can vary considerably. Those in the LRGV are sometimes known as "Boll's Checkerspot," after the southern *bollii* subspecies.

Checkerspots, Patches, and Crescents— Subfamily Nymphalinae

Bordered Patch *Chlosyne lacinia*

The basic pattern on the upperside of the Bordered Patch has a broad orange to yellow band on the hindwing, but it can vary considerably. Most individuals also show a smaller median band and black margins with numerous white spots on the forewing. The underside is similar, except that the white forewing spots are more pronounced. Wingspan: 1.5–2.5 in.

When and Where: Widespread and common year-round. Most numerous in fall when it is attracted to ragweeds and sunflowers, its larval foodplants.

Similar Species: There are no similar LRGV species, although the rare Crimson Patch (*page 133*)—all black with a single large, crimson patch on the hindwing—can appear similar to some variations of the Bordered Patch.

Remarks: Bordered Patch patterns and colors can range from pale- to bright-orange with black markings to almost totally black with only a few white spots.

Checkerspots, Patches, and Crescents—
Subfamily Nymphalinae

Definite Patch *Chlosyne definita*

The upperside is dark brown to black with a trio of red, orange, and red bars on the leading edge, numerous red and orange squares and rectangles that form postmedian and submarginal bands, and broad black margins. The underside of the hindwing is orange with postmedian and marginal bands of black-edged white spots and a connecting white center spot. Wingspan: 1–1.5 in.

When and Where: Common but local, with sporadic populations from July to January. This species can be expected at only a few sites, such as Palo Alto Battlefield. The larval foodplant is stenandrium, a plant of arid, clay soils.

Similar Species: Elada Checkerspot (*page 138*) is most alike, especially the underside, but it is more heavily patterned with orange and red in the basal areas on the upperside. Theona Checkerspot (*page 129*) is somewhat similar but is larger and has a postmedian band of long yellow bars.

Remarks: Pyle's comment that the adults "fly above the thorny vegetation, then perch on the ground with wings spread" is most appropriate.

Checkerspots, Patches, and Crescents— Subfamily Nymphalinae

Banded Patch *Chlosyne endeis*

LRGV specialty. This blackish-brown patch has scattered white forewing spots and a hindwing with a postmedian band of yellow squares and a submarginal band of red patches. The underside is orange-red with a broad white median band edged with black, a narrower basal band, and a series of white marginal crescents on the hindwing. Wingspan: 1.25–1.5 in.

When and Where: Accidental, in March and from October to December. This patch occurs in nearby Mexico, so additional sightings are possible. Larval foodplants include carlowrightia.

Similar Species: Bordered Patch (*page 130*) is somewhat alike but is larger with a wide hindwing band. Definite Patch (*page 131*) is similar in size but lighter and without the scattered white forewing spots.

Remarks: Several authors refer to this species as "Endeis Patch," after its specific scientific name.

Checkerspots, Patches, and Crescents—
Subfamily Nymphalinae

Crimson Patch *Chlosyne janais*

The upperside is coal-black with a large crimson patch in the center of the hindwing and numerous white forewing spots. The fringes are checkered black-and-white. The underside has a similar pattern, but the central hindwing patch is yellow, edged with a series of red squares. There is also a line of yellow submarginal spots. Wingspan: 2–2.5 in.

When and Where: Occasional, most likely in the fall from October to December but also seen in July. The majority of sightings are at flowering shrubs on the floodplain. Larval foodplants include various *Anisacanthus* species.

Similar Species: **Rosita Patch** (*page 134*), a rare stray in the LRGV with historical records only, is smaller, and its central hindwing patch is two-toned, red and yellow. Bordered Patch (*page 130*) can also be similar because it is so varied, but the median band or patch is orange to yellow, not crimson.

Remarks: An extremely large colony exists along Hondo Creek in Medina County, at the southern edge of the Texas Hill Country.

Checkerspots, Patches, and Crescents— Subfamily Nymphalinae

Rosita Patch *Chlosyne rosita*

LRGV specialty. The upperside of the hindwing is coal-black with a large pale-orange central patch, blending to yellow at its base, and numerous white forewing spots. The fringes are checkered black-and-white. The underside of the hindwing has a broad yellowish median band with a reddish outer edge. Wingspan: 1.5–1.75 in.

When and Where: Accidental, with a single historical record in October. Since it does occur in nearby Mexico, additional sightings are possible. Larval foodplants include *Anisacanthus* species.

Similar Species: Crimson Patch (*page 133*) is most alike, but it is larger, the center patch is uniformly bright red, and the underside has large yellow submarginal spots.

Remarks: The Rosita Patch may appear to be a smaller, pale Crimson Patch. Scott refers to this species as "Rosy Patch."

Checkerspots, Patches, and Crescents—
Subfamily Nymphalinae

Red-spotted Patch *Chlosyne marina*

LRGV specialty. The upperside is mostly black with numerous white forewing spots. The hindwing has an irregular yellow median band of elongated spots and a red submarginal spot-band. The underside has a broad yellow median band with black spots on the outer edge, a submarginal row of red ovals, and yellow crescents on the margin. Wingspan: 1.5–1.75 in.

When and Where: Historical records only. Little is known about this patch except for a series of Starr County records in 1973, 1974, 1975, and 1976, all in October, according to Kendall and McGuire (1984). It does occur in nearby Mexico, so additional sightings are possible.

Similar Species: Bordered Patch (*page 130*) can be similar, since it has such varied patterns, but it lacks the red submarginal spot-band.

Remarks: This species is also a rare stray to Arizona, according to Stewart and colleagues (2001). Neck refers to this species as "Yellow Patch."

Checkerspots, Patches, and Crescents— Subfamily Nymphalinae

Elf *Microtia elva*

LRGV specialty. This tiny butterfly is coal-black with a yellow-orange bar across the forewing and an even broader yellow-orange median band on the hindwing and inner edge of the forewing. The underside has a similar pattern but is somewhat paler. Wingspan: .75–1 in.

When and Where: Accidental, recorded only in August. Because it occurs in nearby Mexico, additional sightings are possible. It is most likely to be found in shaded woodlands. Larval foodplants include a member of the Acanthaceae family, tetramerium.

Similar Species: No other black-and-orange LRGV butterfly is so small.

Remarks: This tiny butterfly flies slowly and low to the ground.

Checkerspots, Patches, and Crescents—
Subfamily Nymphalinae

Tiny Checkerspot *Dymasia dymas*

Another tiny butterfly, this one is orange with a matrix of black lines, sometimes faded on the median area of the hindwing, and (usually) a pale bar on the leading edge of the forewing. The underside of the hindwing is pale orange with two bands of black-edged white spots, a lone central spot, and a marginal band of white crescents along a black margin. Wingspan: .75–1.25 in.

When and Where: Rare and local, in October and November. It is most likely to be found in the drier western portion of the LRGV where its larval foodplant, hairy tubetongue, is more abundant.

Similar Species: Elada Checkerspot (*page 138*) is most alike but is generally larger and lacks the pale forewing bar. Its white crescent band on the hindwing underside is located on the inner edge of an orange, rather than black, margin.

Remarks: This species often flies with Elada Checkerspots.

Elada Checkerspot *Texola elada*

A small, active butterfly, its upperside has an orange-and-black checkered pattern, including a submarginal row of orange crescents on the hindwing. The orange underside of the hindwing has three bands of white spots and a lone central spot, all edged with black, and an orange margin. Flight is slow with much flapping. Wingspan: 1–1.25 in.

When and Where: Common but local, from February to December. It is most likely to be found at patches of flowering shrubs in open areas. When found, it usually occurs in numbers, all fluttering about from one flower to another. Larval foodplants include members of the Acanthaceae family, especially anisacanth and tubetongues.

Similar Species: Tiny Checkerspot (*page 137*) is most alike but is smaller, has a pale forewing bar on the upperside, and has a black margin on the hindwing underside. Definite Patch (*page 131*) is also similar but darker with less patterning in the basal areas on the upperside. Vesta Crescent (*page 143*) is similar, too, but lacks the white underwing bands.

Remarks: One of the smaller LRGV butterflies, it is rarely found alone.

Checkerspots, Patches, and Crescents—
Subfamily Nymphalinae

Texan Crescent *Phyciodes texana*

The upperside is mostly black with a narrow median line of white spots across the hindwings, numerous white spots on the forewings, and a mottled red and black basal area. The outer edge of the forewing is indented. The underside of the hindwing is mottled pale-orange, brown, and black and crossed with a pale median band. The trailing edge has pale submarginal crescents. Wingspan: 1.25–1.75 in.

When and Where: Common but local year-round. Texan Crescents are shade-lovers and are usually found along roadsides and trails. They also frequent flowering shrubs in gardens adjacent to shaded areas. Larval foodplants include several members of the Acanthaceae family, including anisacanth, ruellia, and tubetongues.

Similar Species: There are several Mexican crescents with somewhat similar patterns, but the extremely rare **Black Crescent** (*page 141*) is most alike. Its median band is wider and yellow, not white. The **Pale-banded Crescent** (*page 140*) is mostly black with a much wider yellowish median band and a yellowish forewing bar.

Remarks: Texan (*not* Texas) Crescents rarely fly far. Instead, they usually patrol small areas where the same individual can be found on several consecutive days. Males may perch on the ground or on a shrub, waiting for a passing mate.

Checkerspots, Patches, and Crescents—
Subfamily Nymphalinae

Pale-banded Crescent *Phyciodes tulcis*

LRGV specialty. The upperside is mostly black with a moderately wide yellowish median band across the hindwings and scattered yellow spots on the forewings, including a three-spot yellow bar on the leading edge. The band and spots are paler (even white) on females. The underside is pale with a broad whitish median band and a large dark marginal patch with faint crescents. Wingspan: 1.25–1.5 in.

When and Where: Rare and local, in March, May, and from October to December, with most records from the fall months. It is most likely to be found in woodland openings and along trails, especially at Santa Ana NWR and the Valley Nature Center. Larval foodplants include several members of the Acanthaceae family, including dicliptera and ruellia.

Similar Species: Black Crescent (*page 141*) is most alike, but it has reddish basal markings, and its median band is brighter yellow. Texan Crescent (*page 139*) is also similar, but its median band is narrow and white.

Remarks: Many authors refer to this species as "Mexican Crescent."

Checkerspots, Patches, and Crescents— Subfamily Nymphalinae

Black Crescent *Phyciodes ptolyca*

LRGV specialty. This crescent is mostly black on the upperside with a yellow median band across the hindwings and several pale-yellow forewing spots, including a three-spot yellow bar on the leading edge. It also has a distinct indentation on the lower edge of the forewing and reddish basal markings. The underside of the hindwing is mottled with browns and whites, including a pale, S-shaped submarginal spot on the trailing edge. Wingspan: 1.25–1.5 in.

When and Where: Accidental, with single LRGV records in March and December. Because it occurs in nearby Mexico, additional sightings are possible. Larval foodplants are unknown.

Similar Species: Pale-banded Crescent (*page 140*) is most alike, but its yellowish median band is paler. It has pale-spotted fringes, not as evident on Black Crescent. Texan Crescent (*page 139*) is also similar, but the median spot-band is white. It also has pale-spotted fringes.

Remarks: Several authors refer to this species as "False Black Crescent."

Checkerspots, Patches, and Crescents— Subfamily Nymphalinae

Chestnut Crescent *Phyciodes argentea*

LRGV specialty. Sexually dimorphic, the upperside of the male's forewing is mostly chestnut-brown with a network of black basal markings and broad, rounded, black wingtips with tiny white spots. The hindwing has a submarginal band of yellowish crescents. Females are blackish-brown with a submarginal band of yellowish crescents on the hindwing and numerous yellowish forewing spots, including two bars on the leading edge. The underside of the hindwing is reddish-brown with a pale median band. The forewing is also reddish-brown with pale spots. Wingspan: 1.25–1.5 in.

Male

When and Where: Accidental, recorded only in November and December. Since it is fairly common in the nearby Mexican mountains, additional sightings are possible. Larval foodplants are unknown.

Similar Species: Texan Crescent (*page 139*) is somewhat like the female but has a white median band on the hindwing.

Remarks: Most lepidopterists place this species, along with Texan, Pale-banded, and Black crescents, into the genus *Anathanassa*.

Checkerspots, Patches, and Crescents— Subfamily Nymphalinae

Vesta Crescent *Phyciodes vesta*

The upperside is mainly black with numerous orange lines and bars. The forewing has a postmedian band of orange spots, none with dark centers. The hindwing has a median band of orange squares, a postmedian band of orange-edged black spots, and a line of pale submarginal crescents. The underside is pale, with a darker patch on the trailing edge of the hindwing containing pale crescents. Wingspan: .75–1.5 in.

When and Where: Widespread and common year-round. It prefers grassy and brushy sites, only rarely visiting gardens. Larval foodplants include members of the Acanthaceae family, such as hairy tubetongue.

Similar Species: Pearl Crescent (*page 146*) has a broad median band on the upperside of the forewing. Like the Vesta, it has a postmedian band of orange spots, but the two spots nearest the inner margin show dark centers (on most individuals). Phaon Crescent (*page 144*) has a cream-colored median band on the upperside of the forewing. The considerably smaller Elada Checkerspot (*page 138*) has a similar pattern, but its underside has three white bands.

Remarks: Vesta Crescent regularly wanders northward in summer and fall; it has been recorded as far north as Nebraska. Many authorities use the scientific name of *Phyciodes graphica* for this crescent.

Checkerspots, Patches, and Crescents— Subfamily Nymphalinae

Phaon Crescent *Phyciodes phaon*

The upperside of this orange-and-black crescent has a contrasting cream-colored median band on the forewing. The forewing also has a postmedian band of orange spots, with the one nearest the inner margin showing a dark center. The hindwing has a postmedian band of orange-edged black spots and a series of yellowish submarginal crescents. The underside varies from summer to winter, but both forms have one or more white crescents near the center of the hindwing margin. Wingspan: 1–1.5 in.

When and Where: Widespread and common year-round. It frequents open areas, such as roadsides, lawns, and fields, especially areas with frog-fruit, its larval foodplant. It can be abundant at these sites but only rarely visits gardens.

Similar Species: Pearl Crescent (*page 146*) is most alike, but its wider median forewing band is orange. Vesta Crescent (*page 143*) lacks the cream-colored median band; none of the orange spots in its forewing postmedian band have dark centers.

Remarks: With careful searching, the tiny, spiny caterpillars, olive with brown and cream stripes, can sometimes be found on the foodplants.

Summer

Checkerspots, Patches, and Crescents—
Subfamily Nymphalinae

Pearl Crescent *Phyciodes tharos*

The upperside is orange-and-black with a broad, yellow to pale-orange median band on the upperside of the forewing. The forewing also has a postmedian band of orange spots, with the one or two nearest the inner margin showing dark centers (two on most individuals). The hindwing has orange-edged black submarginal spots and broad black-ish margins. The underside is mostly yellow-orange with double pale crescents in the center of the hindwing's trailing edge. Wingspan: 1.25–1.75 in.

When and Where: Widespread and common year-round. It prefers weedy sites, often in shady locations or near wetlands. Larval food-plants include various asters.

Similar Species: Phaon Crescent (*page 144*) is most alike, but the median band on the forewing upperside is narrower and cream colored. Vesta Crescent (*page 143*) is also similar but none of the orange spots in its upperside forewing postmedian band have dark centers.

Remarks: The pattern and color of this crescent can vary considerably.

Anglewings, Ladies, and Buckeyes—Subfamily Nymphalinae

These are medium-sized to large butterflies, many with remarkable colors and patterns. The butterflies in this subfamily feed principally on fruit and sap but occasionally visit flowering plants as well.

Question Mark *Polygonia interrogationis*

This large butterfly has square wingtips and is distinctly marked on the upperside with black spots against a red-orange background on the forewings and, in summer, with velvety black hindwings. In winter, the hindwings are reddish-brown with pale spots. The underside can be lavender-brown to brownish-gray with darker bands and a tiny curved white line with a single white spot (said to resemble a question mark) in the center of the hindwing. Flight is often very fast. Wingspan: 2.25–3 in.

When and Where: Widespread but uncommon year-round. Because its larval foodplants include hackberries, it is most often found in wooded areas, where it may land on a tree trunk, on the ground, on rotting fruit, or even on dung.

Similar Species: No other "commas" occur in the LRGV, so it is unlikely to be confused with any other butterfly. In flight, however, its speed and the orange-red forewing color can be mistaken for those of a leafwing.

Remarks: Perched individuals sometimes sit with wings folded, blending in remarkably well with their surroundings. They feed on fruit and sap, seldom utilizing flower nectar.

Mourning Cloak *Nymphalis antiopa*

This is a subtly beautiful species with velvety maroon wings edged with wide yellowish margins. It has a pair of short yellow bars on the leading edge of the forewing. The underside is charcoal-gray with whitish margins. Wingspan: 2.75–4 in.

When and Where: Accidental, recorded only in April. Since it is widespread throughout the United States, additional sightings are possible. Larval foodplants include hackberries, mulberry, and willows.

Similar Species: No other large North American butterfly has similar features.

Remarks: The name was derived from its rich, velvety appearance, like a cloak worn by mourners.

American Lady *Vanessa virginiensis*

The upperside is mainly pale orange with small, black-edged, blue submarginal dots on the hindwing. The forewing has black rounded wingtips with several white spots and a broad white bar on the leading edge. There is also a tiny white spot in the orange cell just below the black apical area, also visible on the underside. The underside is mottled, with two large eyespots against a brown background on the hindwing. Wingspan: 1.75–2.75 in.

When and Where: Widespread and common year-round. The American Lady is numerous in spring and early summer but often rare in fall. It prefers open, weedy areas with wildflowers but frequents gardens as well. Larval foodplants include a variety of asters.

Similar Species: Painted Lady (*page 152*) is most alike but lacks the tiny white spot in the orange cell below the black apical area on the upperside. It has several smaller eyespots on the underside of the hindwing. West Coast Lady (*page 153*) is also similar but has a square, rather than rounded, wingtip and several black-rimmed, blue submarginal eyespots on the hindwing.

Remarks: This lady is sometimes known as "American Painted Lady."

Painted Lady *Vanessa cardui*

The upperside is reddish with a red-bordered black bar on the leading edge and an extensive black apical area that has several white spots including a white bar on the leading edge. The wingtips are rounded. It has several black submarginal spots on the hindwing. The underside is mottled and has several postmedian eyespots. Wingspan: 2–2.75 in.

When and Where: Widespread and common year-round. It is most abundant during the fall months when southbound migrants reach the Valley. It frequents flowering plants at roadsides and gardens. Larval foodplants include mallows and thistles.

Similar Species: American Lady (*page 151*) is most alike but has a white spot in the orange cell below the black apical area. Its underside has two large eyespots on the hindwing. West Coast Lady (*page 153*) is also similar but has a square, rather than rounded, wingtip and several black-rimmed, blue submarginal eyespots on the hindwing.

Remarks: This is the world's most widespread butterfly; it is absent only from Antarctica, Australia, and New Zealand. As a result, one of its earlier names was "Cosmopolite."

West Coast Lady *Vanessa annabella*

This orange-and-black lady has a squared wingtip, a black apical area with several white spots, and an orange bar on the leading edge. The hindwing has a submarginal row of black-rimmed blue eyespots. The underside is mottled brown and white with several small postmedian eyespots. Wingspan: 1.5–2.25 in.

When and Where: Accidental, recorded only in April and November. It is most likely to be found in gardens. Larval foodplants include mallows.

Similar Species: American (*page 151*) and Painted (*page 152*) ladies are similar, but they have rounded, rather than square, wingtips, and their forewing bars are white instead of orange.

Remarks: The normal range of this western lady barely reaches west Texas.

Red Admiral *Vanessa atalanta*

This *Vanessa* butterfly is well marked on the upperside with a broad red median band across the forewing and a second broad, red marginal band on the hindwing. The large black apical area has several white spots, including a white bar on the leading edge. The underside of the hindwing is mottled brown and black; the red median band is evident only on the forewing. Wingspan: 1.75–3 in.

When and Where: Widespread and common year-round, but most abundant in fall and winter. It feeds at flowering plants along roadsides and in fields and gardens, and it readily comes to bait. Larval foodplants include nettles and pellitories.

Similar Species: No other LRGV butterfly has a similar red-banded pattern.

Remarks: Increased numbers in fall and winter are largely due to immigrants from farther north. This species is sometimes referred to as "the winter butterfly."

Mimic *Hypolimnas misippus*

This medium-sized butterfly is sexually dimorphic. Males are purplish-black on the upperside with a large white patch on both wings and a smaller white apical patch. Females, which resemble Monarchs, are orange-brown with black veins and an extensive black apical area with a band of white bars and a smaller white bar near the wingtip. The underside is pale with similar patterns. Wingspan: 2.25–3.5 in.

When and Where: Accidental, a single August record. Additional records are possible. Larval foodplants include various species of mallows and members of the Anacantheae family.

Similar Species: Males are unique and are unlikely to be confused with any other species; females are somewhat like Monarchs (*page 210*) but have a more extensive black apical area.

Remarks: Entomologists believe that this species is African in origin and was introduced into the Americas during the slave trade. Or, it may have been brought to the West Indies and then immigrated to Florida, where it has been recorded on several occasions.

Common Buckeye *Junonia coenia*

The upperside has one large and one small gold-rimmed eyespot on both forewing and hindwing. The large forewing eyespot is mostly surrounded with a whitish area that extends in a wide bar to the leading edge. Also, two black-edged red bars are present on the leading edge of the forewing. The underside of the hindwing is mottled gray-brown in spring but reddish by fall. It flaps and glides in flight. Wingspan: 2–2.75 in.

When and Where: Widespread and common year-round. This lovely butterfly prefers open areas, including roadways. Larval foodplants are varied, including several members of the Acanthaceae family (such as anisacanth), the Plantaginaceae family (such as plantains), and the Scrophulariaceae family (including snapdragons).

Similar Species: Tropical (*page 158*) and Mangrove (*page 159*) buck-eyes are most alike, but the area that circles the eyespots and the bars that extend to the leading edge of the forewing are pinkish or pale orange instead of white.

Remarks: Much research is necessary to fully understand the relationships between the buckeyes.

Spring

Fall

Anglewings, Ladies, and Buckeyes—Subfamily Nymphalinae

Tropical Buckeye *Junonia evarete*

Like the Common Buckeye, the Tropical Buckeye has two eyespots on each wing, but the inner edge of the larger forewing eyespot is brown, not whitish. A pinkish bar extends from the outer edge of the eyespot to the leading edge, outside two black-edged, red bars. The underside is brown with two small, blue-centered postmedian eyespots. Wingspan: 1.5–2.5 in.

J. e. nigrosuffusa

When and Where: Widespread but rare year-round. It is occasionally found feeding at flowering plants along roadsides and in gardens. Larval foodplants include black mangroves and lippia.

Similar Species: Mangrove Buckeye (*page 159*) is most alike, but the large forewing eyespot is surrounded by pale orange. Common Buckeye (*page 156*) is also similar, but the large forewing eyespot is surrounded by white.

Remarks: There is also a dark form (subspecies *nigrosuffusa*) that is most likely to be found near the coast. This melanistic form is darker overall with less distinct markings. The specific scientific names of Tropical and Mangrove buckeyes have been switched by some authors. Much research is still needed on these two species.

Mangrove Buckeye *Junonia genoveva*

The upperside is rich brown with a pair of eyespots on both wings. The larger forewing eyespot has a blue center but is mostly black and is surrounded by pale orange that extends in a narrow bar to the leading edge. There are also two black-edged, red bars on the leading edge. The hindwing has a pair of black-edged brown eyespots with blue centers. The underside is rusty with a pale median band and two small, white-edged, blue eyespots. Wingspan: 1.5–2.5 in.

When and Where: Rare and local, found only near the coast at scattered times of the year—March, April, October, and November. Larval foodplants are limited to black mangroves.

Similar Species: Tropical Buckeye (*page 158*) is most alike, but the inner edge of the large forewing eyespot is brown and the bar extending to the leading edge is pinkish. Common Buckeye (*page 156*) is similar, but the inner edge of the large forewing spot and the bar that extends to the leading edge are white.

Remarks: The majority of Mangrove Buckeyes found at stands of black mangroves are melanistic, like "dark" Tropical Buckeyes. The entire buckeye complex is poorly understood.

White Peacock *Anartia jatrophae*

LRGV specialty. One of the few mostly white butterflies in the LRGV, the upperside has a black-bordered blue-gray bar on the leading edge and one oblong black median spot on the forewing. The hindwing has two smaller round postmedian spots. The scalloped margins are pale orange with a black submarginal line. The underside is similar but tan. Flight is usually slow and direct. Wingspan: 2–2.75 in.

When and Where: Widespread and common year-round. This tropical butterfly prefers open areas, spending considerable time on the ground. It utilizes a wide variety of larval foodplants, ranging from lippia and ruellia to frog-fruit.

Similar Species: The smaller Checkered White (*page 41*) is also white but has dark squares; it can hardly be confused with this more colorful species.

Remarks: This species wanders northward in summer and fall, sometimes colonizing wetland areas.

Banded Peacock *Anartia fatima*

LRGV specialty. The Banded Peacock has a contrasting upperside pattern, with a blackish apical area with scattered yellowish or whitish spots, a reddish-brown basal area with four red spots on the hindwing, and a broad yellow or white band across both wings. The underside is reddish-brown with a pale median band. Flight is usually slow and soaring. Wingspan: 2.5–3 in.

When and Where: Rare, from March to January. A tropical species, it is most often found in gardens and at flowering plants in or close to shaded areas. Larval foodplants include members of the Acanthaceae family, including justica and ruellia.

Similar Species: It cannot be confused with any other North American butterfly.

Remarks: Because the Banded Peacock is so abundant throughout most of Mexico, it's strange that it's not more common in the LRGV.

Anglewings, Ladies, and Buckeyes—Subfamily Nymphalinae

Malachite *Siproeta stelenes*

LRGV specialty. One of the Valley's most outstanding species, it is easily recognized by its large size, black-and-green pattern above, and brown, green, and yellow below. The upperside has extensive greenish patches bordered with black, including a broad median band, large oblong patches near the wingtips, and a line of postmedian spots on the hindwing. It also has a short black tail-like projection on the hindwing. Males are brighter than females. Flight is usually slow and gliding. Wingspan: 3.25–4 in.

When and Where: Widespread but occasional year-round, recorded most often in fall, usually at gardens and in shaded areas. In the tropics, larval foodplants include several members of the Acanthaceae family, such as justica and ruellia.

Similar Species: No other large butterfly could possibly be confused with this incredible creature.

Remarks: It feeds on various overripe fruit, especially mangos and bananas.

Rusty-tipped Page *Siproeta epaphus*

LRGV specialty. The upperside is sharply divided by a band of white squares that extend from the leading edge of the forewing to near the trailing edge of the hindwing. The basal portion of the wings is rusty-brown to dark brown, the outer portion orange. The hindwing margin is deeply scalloped, with one short tail-like projection. The underside has similar features. Wingspan: 2.75–3.5 in.

When and Where: Accidental, recorded only once in November. This gorgeous butterfly is fairly common in nearby Mexico, so additional sightings are possible. Larval foodplants include tropical members of the Acanthaceae family.

Similar Species: No other LRGV butterfly has a similar pattern.

Remarks: In Mexico, this species usually perches on high foliage, waiting for a passing mate.

Admirals, Bluewings, Crackers, and Daggerwings—Subfamily Limenitidinae

These medium-sized to large butterflies have varied shapes and unusual individual characteristics. Most feed only on fruit and sap.

Red-spotted Purple *Limenitis arthemis*

The upperside is primarily black with deep blue on the outer half of the hindwing that is divided by a solid black submarginal band. The forewing has small red apical spots and a submarginal series of short white lines. The underside of the hindwing is bluish with reddish cells, three large, black-edged, red basal spots, and seven red submarginal spots. The forewing is reddish with a blue base and two black-edged red bars. Wingspan: 3–3.5 in.

When and Where: Accidental, a single November record. Because this species does reside in nearby Mexico, as well as in northeastern and west Texas, additional sightings are possible.

Similar Species: No other LRGV butterfly has a similar pattern and combination of colors.

Remarks: The lone record of this species is of the western subspecies. This butterfly is sometimes referred to as "Red-spotted Admiral."

Admirals, Bluewings, Crackers, and Daggerwings— Subfamily Limenitidinae

Viceroy *Limenitis archippus*

Like the Monarch, the Viceroy is deep orange with numerous black veins, but the majority of North American Viceroys also have a curved black postmedian band across the hindwings, evident from above and below. The Mexican subspecies lacks the all-black hindwing band. Instead, the band is narrow and broken by scattered white spots. Flight is usually swift with considerable gliding. Wingspan: 2.75–3.25 in.

When and Where: Very rare and local along the Rio Grande River and at ponds, from April to November. Larval foodplants are limited to willows that generally grow only in moist soils.

Similar Species: Monarch (*page 210*) is most alike but is larger and lacks the all-black or white-spotted postmedian band on the hindwing.

Remarks: It probably was more numerous in the past, before so much of the Rio Grande floodplain was impacted by agriculture and grazing.

Admirals, Bluewings, Crackers, and Daggerwings—Subfamily Limenitidinae

Band-celled Sister *Adelpha fessonia*

LRGV specialty. The upperside is brown with a broad white median band that extends from the leading edge of the forewing and crosses both wings, a large gold patch on the rounded wingtip, and a wide brown margin containing three black bands. It also has a gold spot on the inner edge of the hindwing. The underside is reddish-brown with the white median band and with white and pale-brown basal streaks. Flight is usually slow with much gliding. Wingspan: 2.25–2.75 in.

When and Where: Rare, reported every month but May and June. Most records are from gardens. Larval foodplants are limited to hackberries.

Similar Species: **Spot-celled Sister** (*page 169*) is very similar, but the white median band does not extend to the leading edge of the forewing. Female **Pavon** (*page 202*) and **Silver** (*page 204*) **emperors** are also similar, but they have squared wingtips. The white median band does not reach the leading edge of the forewing on either species.

Remarks: Some sight reports of this rare species may actually be one of the two similar emperors.

Admirals, Bluewings, Crackers, and Daggerwings— Subfamily Limenitidinae

California Sister *Adelpha bredowii*

The upperside is dark brown or black with a white median spot-band that extends across the wings, tapering toward the inner margin of the hindwing. The spot-band is broken on the forewing. The forewing also has a large orange apical patch and a white three-spot bar on the leading edge. The underside is lilac-brown with a white median band and reddish basal spots. Wingspan: 2.75–3.25 in.

When and Where: Accidental, a single November record. Since this species is fairly common in oak woodlands to the west and north-west in Texas, additional sightings are possible. Larval foodplants are limited to oaks.

Similar Species: **Band-celled Sister** (*page 167*) and **Spot-celled Sister** (*page 169*) are somewhat alike, but they are brown with an unbroken median band that extends to or very near the leading edge of the forewing. Both are generally smaller than California Sister.

Remarks: Some authors refer to this species as "Arizona Sister"; the lone Valley record was the Arizona subspecies *eulalia*, instead of the California form.

Admirals, Bluewings, Crackers, and Daggerwings—Subfamily Limenitidinae

Spot-celled Sister *Adelpha basiloides*

LRGV specialty. The upperside of the blackish-brown wings has a broad white median band that does not extend to the leading edge of the forewing. A large golden apical patch is located just inside the rounded wingtip. The wide brown margins contain two black forewing bands and three hindwing bands. It also has a gold spot on the inner edge of the hindwing. The underside has a similar median band, but the remainder is pale with numerous brown bands. Wingspan: 2.25–2.5 in.

When and Where: Accidental, a single record in November. Since this species does occur in nearby Mexico, additional sightings are possible. Larval foodplants include various members of the madder family, none of which are known in the United States.

Similar Species: **Band-celled Sister** (*page 167*) is most alike, but the white median band extends to the leading edge of the forewing. Female **Pavon** (*page 202*) and **Silver** (*page 204*) **emperors** are also similar but have squared wingtips.

Remarks: This is the rarest of the five similar species. Neck refers to this species as "Tropical Sister" and Band-celled Sister as "Mexican Sister." Mexico has twenty species of sisters (*Adelpha*).

Common Banner *Epiphile adrasta*

LRGV specialty. The underside of perched individuals is mainly rusty-brown with four eyespots on the hindwing and a pair of yellowish bands at least partially visible on the forewing. The wingtips are square. The seldom-seen upperside is dull to bright orange with a broad black median band, a black apical area, and a black basal area. The wingtip is orange on males and black on females. Wingspan: 2.25–2.75 in.

When and Where: Rare, from October to January. It is most likely at overripe fruit or bait, and it perches on tree trunks for extended periods. Larval foodplants include soapberry vines, such as serjania.

Similar Species: No other butterfly has a similar color pattern.

Remarks: Some authors refer to this tropical species as "Dimorphic Bark Wing," due to its cryptic underwing pattern.

Admirals, Bluewings, Crackers, and Daggerwings—Subfamily Limenitidinae

Mexican Bluewing *Myscelia ethusa*

LRGV specialty. This is a spectacular butterfly on the upperside, with deep-blue parallel bands across black wings, numerous white apical spots, and square wingtips. The underside is mottled brown and black, making it difficult to detect when perched. Flight is swift, and it usually returns to perch on a tree trunk or branch. Wingspan: 2.5–3.25 in.

When and Where: Uncommon and local in shaded woodlands year-round, less numerous in winter. It rarely flies in the open, and when it does, it remains close to shaded areas. The only known larval foodplant in the LRGV is Vasey adelia.

Similar Species: Blackened Bluewing (*page 172*) is possible, although there are no recent records. It is similar, but the upper forewings are mostly black with much smaller white apical spots.

Remarks: No other LRGV butterfly so represents the semi-tropical woodlands.

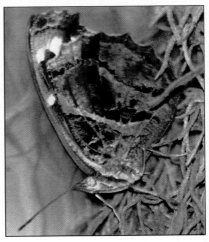

Admirals, Bluewings, Crackers, and Daggerwings—Subfamily Limenitidinae

Blackened Bluewing *Myscelia cyananthe*

The underside of the hindwing is mottled with browns and black, but the forewing has a broad, uneven, black band below a pale apical area. The wingtips are square. The upperside is primarily black with a deep-blue median band across the hindwing, a blue base on the forewing, and white apical spots. Wingspan: 2–2.25 in.

When and Where: Accidental, with an historical record in October. This species is reasonably common in nearby Mexico, so additional sightings are possible. Larval foodplants include members of the Euphorbiaceae family.

Similar Species: **Mexican Bluewing** (*page 171*) is most alike but has several parallel, blue bands on the upperside of the wings and large white spots on the apical areas.

Remarks: This species is also a rare stray in Arizona and California.

Dingy Purplewing *Eunica monima*

LRGV specialty. The underside is pale brown with darker median streaks and three indistinct postmedian eyespots, a large one and a smaller pair directly below. The wingtip is rounded. The upperside, though only occasionally seen, is deep purplish-brown with several contrasting white forewing spots. Flight is swift and often difficult to follow. Wingspan: 1.75–2 in.

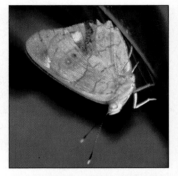

When and Where: Occasional, from June to November. It usually perches on woody plants with closed wings. It feeds on overripe fruit, including that found at bait stations. Larval foodplants include gumbo limbo, found only south of the border.

Similar Species: Florida Purplewing (*page 174*) is very similar, but the underside is darker brown. It has an obvious concave notch below the tip of the forewing.

Remarks: This species occasionally wanders northward into central Texas in summer. For more information, see my 2003 article listed in Appendix 2, References.

Admirals, Bluewings, Crackers, and Daggerwings— Subfamily Limenitidinae

Florida Purplewing *Eunica tatila*

The underside of the hindwing is mottled brown with faint eyespots. The forewing has several white and black spots and a concave notch below the tip. The upperside is blackish-brown, with a purplish wash over all except the marginal areas, and has several large white forewing spots. Wingspan: 1.5–2.5 in.

When and Where: Accidental, from August to October. It occurs in nearby Mexico, so additional sightings are possible. It is most likely at overripe fruit or at bait stations. Like the Dingy Purplewing, it perches on woody plants for long periods of time.

Similar Species: **Dingy Purplewing** (*page 173*) is most alike but is generally smaller, with a paler underside. The tips of its forewings are not notched.

Remarks: Many authors refer to this species as "Mexican Purplewing." It is resident in south Florida, hence its name.

Admirals, Bluewings, Crackers, and Daggerwings—Subfamily Limenitidinae

Blue-eyed Sailor *Dynamine dyonis*

LRGV specialty. The underside is almost gaudy with its white, rust, and blue pattern, including a pair of rusty-edged blue eyespots surrounded by white in the center of the hindwing. The basal area is white with rusty streaks. The upperside is brown with a broad white median band in females, but males are golden-green with blackish bars and margins. Wingspan: 1.5–1.75 in.

When and Where: Rare and local, in June and from September to December. It is most likely to be found at or near noseburn, its larval foodplant, which occurs in woodland areas, such as at Santa Ana NWR.

Similar Species: No other LRGV butterfly comes close to resembling this oddly marked little creature.

Remarks: During October and November 2003, several individuals were recorded at or near Santa Ana NWR, where egg-laying that may lead to colonization was recorded.

Female

Male

Admirals, Bluewings, Crackers, and Daggerwings— Subfamily Limenitidinae

Common Mestra *Mestra amymone*

A small, gray-white butterfly with a pale-orange trailing edge on the hindwing and brownish-gray tips and margins on the forewing. The underside is pale orange except for white spots that form a necklace on the hindwing and white streaks on the forewing. Flight is slow and weak. Wingspan: 1.5–2 in.

When and Where: Widespread and common year-round. It is most numerous in fall. Larval foodplants include noseburn.

Similar Species: The size and color pattern of this little butterfly is unique.

Remarks: Its earlier name was "Amymone." A resident in most of south Texas, it regularly wanders northward in late summer and fall and has been recorded as far north as Nebraska.

Admirals, Bluewings, Crackers, and Daggerwings— Subfamily Limenitidinae

Red Rim *Biblis hyperia*

LRGV specialty. The upperside of this large butterfly is velvety black except for paler marginal areas on the forewings and a broad, uneven, bright-red band across the scalloped hindwings. The underside is gray-brown, lighter on the outer portion of the forewing, with a pinkish postmedian band and three small red basal spots on the hindwing. Wingspan: 2.25–2.75 in.

When and Where: Occasional and local in woodland areas, with records from March, May, and from July to December. Most records are in fall. It was recorded at several locations in 2003.

Similar Species: No other LRGV butterfly has black wings with a bright-red hindwing band.

Remarks: Although it looks very much like a tailless swallowtail, Red Rims are more closely related to admirals and crackers.

Admirals, Bluewings, Crackers, and Daggerwings— Subfamily Limenitidinae

Red Cracker *Hamadryas amphinome*

LRGV specialty. The upperside is blackish with numerous blue markings and a broad whitish bar on the leading edge of the forewing. The hindwing is dominated by large submarginal teardrops with white or blue centers. The underside of the hindwing has an extensive reddish base. The forewing underside has a broad white median band and smaller spots. Both wings have white marginal spots. Wingspan: 3.25–3.5 in.

When and Where: Accidental, with records from January and September. Since it occurs in nearby Mexico, additional sightings are possible. It is most likely to be found at overripe fruit, tree sap, and bait stations or perched on nearby tree trunks. Larval foodplants in the tropics include Euphorbiaceae vines; local species are unknown.

Similar Species: **Guatemalan Cracker** (*page 186*) is most alike on the underside of the hindwing, but the extensive basal area is yellowish instead of reddish. It has a black-edged reddish forewing bar surrounded with white.

Remarks: The cracker name was derived from the cracking sounds made by the wings in flight, utilized by males "to communicate with each other," according to Scott. Perched individuals have a tendency to walk in short spurts.

Admirals, Bluewings, Crackers, and Daggerwings—Subfamily Limenitidinae

Gray Cracker *Hamadryas februa*

LRGV specialty. Although the overall color of the upperside is grayish-brown, the abundant spots and bars vary from white to black and include a wavy reddish bar, edged with black, on the leading edge of the forewing. The hindwing has several submarginal eyespots that are edged with (head to tail) orange, black, and brown. The underside has an extensive pale base, numerous submarginal eyespots edged with black and orange, and a checkered white-and-brown fringe. Flight is swift and high, usually ending with a return to the same or an adjacent tree trunk or area of sap. Wingspan: 2.75–3.5 in.

When and Where: Occasional, from July to December, but recorded most years. The majority of sightings are at tree sap or bait stations. Larval foodplants include members of the Euphorbiaceae family, such as noseburn.

Similar Species: **Variable** (*page 184*) and **Guatemalan** (*page 186*) **crackers** are somewhat similar. The upperside of Variable Cracker has blue-rimmed black submarginal eyespots and blue-rimmed patches on the forewing. Guatemalan Cracker is larger, with black-rimmed blue submarginal eyespots.

Remarks: All the crackers are similar, except for a few key features. There is a good discussion of these characteristics in an article entitled "Cracking the Code" by Jeffrey Glassberg, which is listed in Appendix 2, References.

Admirals, Bluewings, Crackers, and Daggerwings—Subfamily Limenitidinae

Variable Cracker *Hamadryas feronia*

LRGV specialty. This grayish-blue cracker has several large pale forewing cells, along with an S-shaped, black-edged, reddish bar on the leading edge. The hindwing has a yellowish bar on the leading edge and several submarginal eyespots with white centers edged in blue on the trailing edge. The underside has an extensive yellowish base, a series of black submarginal rings, and a black-and-white fringe on the hindwing. Wingspan: 2.75–3.25 in.

When and Where: Accidental, recorded from October to December. This species is fairly common in nearby Mexico, so additional sightings are possible. It is most likely to be found at overripe fruit, at bait stations, or perched on an adjacent tree trunk. Larval foodplants are viny eupatoriums.

Similar Species: Guatemalan Cracker (*page 186*) is most alike but is larger, has a distinct white spot on the leading edge of the forewing, and has submarginal eyespots that are black-ringed with a pair of concentric white rings. **Gray Cracker** (*page 182*) is similar but has submarginal eyespots edged with orange, black, and brown.

Remarks: All the crackers commonly perch head-down on tree trunks.

Admirals, Bluewings, Crackers, and Daggerwings— Subfamily Limenitidinae

Guatemalan Cracker *Hamadryas guatemalena*

LRGV specialty. The largest of the LRGV crackers, the upperside has extensive bluish-gray areas with pale oblong spots, many blackish bars and streaks, and a distinct white spot on the leading edge of the forewing. It also has a black-edged reddish bar on the leading edge of the forewing, and there are several black-ringed submarginal eyespots and a pair of concentric white rings on the hindwing. The underside has a pale yellow base, numerous round, white submarginal spots on the hindwing, and a forewing with numerous white spots and patches, including a distinguishing white spot on the leading edge just below the wingtip. Wingspan: 3–4 in.

When and Where: Accidental, recorded in August and from October to February. It is fairly common in nearby Mexico, so additional sightings are possible. It is most likely to be found at overripe fruit and tree sap. Larval foodplants are unknown north of the border but are probably viny eupatorium species.

Similar Species: The grayish-blue **Variable Cracker** (*page 184*) is most alike, but its hindwing eyespots have a white center spot and a single bluish rim. The underside of the **Red Cracker** (*page 180*) is similar, but the basal area is reddish. The underside of the **Gray Cracker** (*page 182*) is also similar, but the eyespots are edged with black and orange.

Remarks: All the crackers can look alike in less-than-ideal light, but a careful examination of their submarginal hindwing eyespots provides the best clue for identification. Scott refers to this species as "South American Cracker."

Orion Cecropian *Historis odius*

A large, leafwing-like butterfly with an elongated forewing and pointed hindwing. The underside of the hindwing is pale orange to purplish-brown and looks leaf-like, making the butterfly difficult to see when perched. The upperside is mostly black with an extensive orange patch on the forewing and a white teardop on the black apical area. The orange also extends onto the basal portion of the hindwing. Wingspan: 4.5–4.75 in.

When and Where: Accidental, with an historical record in July. Since it does occur in nearby Mexico, additional sightings are possible. Larval foodplants include various cecropias, not native to the United States.

Similar Species: No other large butterfly has similar features.

Remarks: This species also occurs as a stray in Florida.

Admirals, Bluewings, Crackers, and Daggerwings— Subfamily Limenitidinae

Blomfild's Beauty *Smyrna blomfildia*

LRGV specialty. The underside of the hindwing is mostly dark brown to black with numerous whitish circles and lines and a series of sub-marginal eyespots. The seldom-seen upperside is sexually dimorphic. The male is mostly rusty with broad black wingtips crossed by three white spots. The female is rusty-brown with a yellow median band on the forewing and black wingtips with three white spots. The antennae are long and have an orange tip on the otherwise black club. Wingspan: 3–3.25 in.

When and Where: Accidental, from November to January. This species is reasonably common in nearby Mexico, so additional sightings are possible. It is most likely to be found at overripe fruit or bait stations or perched on nearby tree trunks. Larval foodplants include nettles.

Similar Species: No other LRGV butterfly has a similar complicated underwing pattern, although Karwinski's Beauty (*Smyrna karwinskii*) is found in nearby Mexico and could possibly be seen in the LRGV. It has a paler hindwing on the upperside and only one black tail-like projection.

Remarks: In the tropics, this and the closely related Karwinski's Beauty move into the higher mountains where they aestivate during the dry season.

Admirals, Bluewings, Crackers, and Daggerwings—
Subfamily Limenitidinae

Waiter Daggerwing *Marpesia coresia*

LRGV specialty. The upperside is chocolate-brown with rusty margins. It has square, slightly falcate wingtips and long tails. The underside is two-tone with an ivory basal area and a reddish-brown outer half. Wingspan: 2–2.5 in.

When and Where: Accidental, in July. It is uncommon in nearby Mexico, but additional sightings are possible. Larval foodplants are unknown.

Similar Species: Although **Ruddy** (*page 194*) and **Many-banded** (*page 192*) **daggerwings** are similar in size and shape, both are streaked on the upperside.

Remarks: Some authors refer to this species simply as "Waiter."

Many-banded Daggerwing *Marpesia chiron*

LRGV specialty. The upperside of this long-tailed butterfly is dark brown with numerous broad orange-brown stripes running from near the leading edge of the forewing across the wings. It has pale spots in the apical area, square wingtips, and brown-edged black squares near the tail. The underside is divided in two, with purplish-brown on the outer half and a paler brown with gray bands on the basal half. Wingspan: 2.5–2.75 in.

When and Where: Occasional, in February, April, and from July to October, most likely in fall. It can occur almost anywhere but prefers shaded areas. Larval foodplants are limited to figs.

Similar Species: **Ruddy Daggerwing** (*page 194*) has a similar shape but is orange-red with brown stripes. **Waiter Daggerwing** (*page 191*) is also similar, although there are no recent records. It is dark brown on the upperside, except for rusty margins, and has two-toned underparts—ivory on the basal half and reddish-brown on the outer half.

Remarks: Daggerwings have a rather bizarre appearance, with their strange shape and long tails.

Ruddy Daggerwing *Marpesia petreus*

LRGV specialty. The upperside of this large, orange-red butterfly has three narrow brown stripes between the leading edge of the forewing and the tail area. It has a long orange tail and a second much shorter one. The underside is mainly brown with two dark bands. Flight is swift and straight. Wingspan: 2.5–3 in.

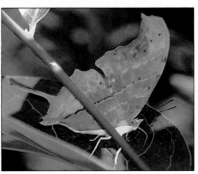

When and Where: Occasional, in February, April, and from July to November, most often reported in summer and fall. It feeds on overripe fruit and bait, but it also frequents flowering plants. Larval foodplants in Mexico consist of fig leaves.

Similar Species: **Many-banded Daggerwing** (*page 192*) is similar in shape but is brown with several orange-brown stipes.

Remarks: Scott refers to this species as "Red Dagger Wing."

Leafwings—Subfamily Charaxinae

Leafwings are medium-sized to large butterflies that have bright, colorful uppersides but dull underwings that provide marvelous camouflage when perched. They can look very much like dead leaves. Wingtips are falcate. Flight is extremely fast and often difficult to follow.

Tropical Leafwing *Anaea aidea*

The underside, most often visible, is mottled gray and black with one prominent tail-like projection and a second very short projection on the scalloped hindwing. The upperside is orange-red with several brown-rimmed yellowish submarginal spots (most evident on females) and a black horizontal streak and vertical bar near the leading edge of the forewing. Wingspan: 2.5–3.25 in.

When and Where: Common but local year-round. A butterfly of wooded areas, most often found along shaded roadways and trails. Leafwings obtain nutrients from fruit, sap, and dung, but they rarely feed on nectar. Larval foodplants include various crotons.

Similar Species: Goatweed Leafwing (*page 196*) is most alike, but the hindwing edge is smooth with a single tail-like projection.

Remarks: This is the most common of the four species of leafwings that have been recorded in the LRGV.

Leafwings—Subfamily Charaxinae

Goatweed Leafwing *Anaea andria*

Perched individuals have a grayish-purple to brown underside, with a single tail-like projection on the otherwise smooth hindwing edge. The upperside of males is reddish-orange and unmarked, but females are somewhat paler with a wide, black-rimmed, yellowish submarginal band on the forewing that extends a short distance onto the hindwing. The female also has a short black forewing bar. Wingspan: 2.5–3.25 in.

When and Where: Uncommon and local in and adjacent to wooded areas, from March through December. This leafwing feeds on over-ripe fruit and sap. Like the other leafwings, it regularly perches on woody plants. Larval foodplants consist of crotons, including goatweed, from whence its name was derived.

Similar Species: Tropical Leafwing (*page 195*) is most alike but is readily separated when perched by its scalloped hindwing margin and two tail-like projections.

Remarks: Goatweed Leafwing is resident throughout Texas and beyond.

Angled Leafwing *Anaea glycerium*

When perched, this leafwing shows a long, angled hindwing with a broad tail-like projection. The underside is pale orange and mottled with blackish lines. The upperside is bright orange with a large dark apical arc. Wingspan: 2.25–3.25 in.

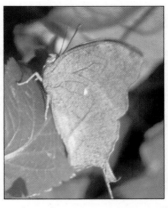

When and Where: Accidental, with single records from July and August. It is fairly common in nearby Mexico, so additional sightings are possible. It is most likely to be found at overripe fruit or bait stations. Larval foodplants are limited to crotons.

Similar Species: None of the other leafwings has such a long, angled shape.

Remarks: Some authors refer to this species as "Crinkled Leafwing," due to its underwing appearance. This species is also a rare stray to southern Arizona.

Pale-spotted Leafwing *Anaea pithyusa*

LRGV specialty. The underside is dark gray-brown, darkest on the hindwing and basal portion of the forewing. There are pale patches on the center of the forewing, including a faint reddish spot. The trailing portion of the hindwing has two black spots in front of a short tail-like projection. The upperside is blackish, with a bluish-green wash and several large, white or blue forewing spots. Wingspan: 2.25–3 in.

When and Where: Rare, in March and from July to January. This species is fairly common in nearby Mexico, so additional sightings are possible. Larval foodplants include crotons.

Similar Species: No other LRGV leafwing has such a dark upperside.

Remarks: Because of its deep-bluish upperside, it sometimes is known as "Blue Leafwing."

Emperors—Subfamily Apaturinae

These are medium-sized, primarily brown, black, and white butterflies that utilize hackberry foliage as their larval foodplant. They all have eyespots and long antennae. Males often perch on high foliage and wait for passing mates. They are fast fliers and very territorial. They take nectar from flowers but also obtain nutrients from sap, fruit, and dung.

Hackberry Emperor *Asterocampa celtis*

The upperside is brown to orange-brown with darker apical areas that have numerous white spots. The forewing has one or two submarginal eyespots and two dark bars on the leading edge; the outer bar is complete, but the inner one is broken. The hindwing has several black submarginal spots. The underside is pale with similar features. Wingspan: 1.5–2.5 in.

When and Where: Common but local, from March to December. It is rarely found any distance from woodlands with hackberry trees. It seldom occurs in abundance.

Similar Species: Tawny Emperor (*page 201*) and Empress Leilia (*page 200*) are similar but differ in subtle ways. Tawny Emperor lacks upperside forewing eyespots and has two unbroken bars on the leading edge of the forewing. Empress Leilia has upperside forewing eyespots but has, like the Tawny, two unbroken bars on the leading edge of the forewing.

Remarks: The specific scientific name is derived from the genus of hackberry trees (*Celtis*).

Empress Leilia *Asterocampa leilia*

Usually the brightest of the three hackberry butterflies, it is deep brown to orange on the upperside with blackish apical areas that have numerous white spots. The forewing has submarginal eyespots, as well as two solid, dark bars on the leading edge. The hindwing has several submarginal eyespots. The underside is pale with similar features. Wingspan: 1.5–2.5 in.

When and Where: Common but local, from February to December. It is most numerous in hackberry woodlands, perched on the higher vegetation, but it also commonly perches on roadways and trails.

Similar Species: Hackberry (*page 199*) and Tawny (*page 201*) emperors are very similar and are best separated by eyespots and leading-edge bars on the forewing upperside. Hackberry has eyespots but one of its leading-edge bars is broken. Tawny lacks eyespots on the forewing.

Remarks: Empress Leilia spends more time on the ground than the other hackberry butterflies.

Emperors—Subfamily Apaturinae

Tawny Emperor *Asterocampa clyton*

The upperside is pale orange-brown (tawny), although much darker and paler individuals are occasionally recorded. The forewing lacks any eyespots but does have a pair of unbroken black bars on the leading edge of the forewing. The hindwing has several submarginal eyespots. The underside is pale with similar features. Wingspan: 1.5–2.75 in.

When and Where: Common but local, from April to February. Another butterfly of the hackberry woodlands, it can usually be found in numbers. When fresh sap is available, dozens may gather in close association to feed.

Similar Species: Hackberry Emperor (*page 199*) and Empress Leilia (*page 200*) are most alike, but both have eyespots on the forewing.

Remarks: This is the most common of the three *Asterocampa* species.

Emperors—Subfamily Apaturinae

Pavon Emperor *Doxocopa pavon*

LRGV specialty. Sexually dimorphic, the upperside of females is marked by a broad white median band that extends from near the inner margin of the hindwing to just below a gold patch near the square wingtip. The male is deep purple (blue-purple with a silvery median band in good light) with a pair of orange patches near the wingtip. The inner margin of the hindwing is pale orange. The underside of both sexes is mottled brown and gray with two solid, black bars on the leading edge of the forewing. Wingspan: 1.75–2.75 in.

Female

Male

When and Where: Rare, in May and from August to December. It is absent most years. Since it is fairly common in nearby Mexico, additional sightings are possible. Several females were present at Santa Ana NWR during October and November 2003.

Similar Species: **Silver Emperor** (*page 204*), especially the female, is similar to the female Pavon. It is slightly larger, has a short tail projection, and is whitish on the underside. **Band-celled** (*page 167*) and **Spot-celled** (*page 169*) **sisters** are also similar to female Pavon Emperor, but both have rounded wingtips. Also, their white median bands extend to or nearly to the leading edge of the forewing.

Remarks: The striking difference in color and pattern betweeen males and females is exceptional.

Emperors—Subfamily Apaturinae

Silver Emperor *Doxocopa laure*

LRGV specialty. Like the Pavon Emperor, the Silver Emperor is sexually dimorphic, although both sexes are dark brown with square wingtips. The male's upperside has a broad white median band on the hindwing that widens into a gold band on the forewing and extends to the leading edge. The female's all-white median band does not extend to the edge, and a separate gold square is situated just below the wingtip. Hindwing margins are scalloped with a very short tail projection. The underside of the hindwing is whitish, but a pale rendition of the upperside pattern is visible on the forewing. Wingspan: 2–2.75 in.

When and Where: Rare, from July to December. It is fairly common in nearby Mexico, so additional sightings are possible. It frequents flowering plants on the floodplain or in nearby gardens. Larval foodplants also include hackberry foliage.

Similar Species: The female **Pavon Emperor** (*page 202*) is smaller, has a narrower white median band, and lacks any semblence of a tail. **Band-celled** (*page 167*) and **Spot-celled** (*page 169*) **sisters** have rounded, instead of square, wingtips, and their white median bands extend to or nearly to the leading edge of the forewing.

Remarks: The specific scientific name "*laure*" is sometimes used as a common name for this tropical species.

Satyrs—Subfamily Satyrinae

Satyrs, small to medium-sized butterflies, are predominantly brown with one or more marginal eyespots. The costal vein has a swollen base. Flight is usually low to the ground and exhibits a distinct bouncing or "hopping" pattern.

Gemmed Satyr *Cyllopsis gemma*

The underside of this little nondescript butterfly is all brown, except for three faint, wavy median lines and an oblong gray patch with three tiny, shiny, blue spots on the hindwing margin. The upperside, though rarely seen, is light brown with a reddish wash and unmarked. Wingspan: 1–1.5 in.

When and Where: Common but local year-round. This is a woodland butterfly that can be quite numerous at times. It rarely, if ever, visits flowers in open areas, but it is attracted to fruit and bait. Larval foodplants are limited to grasses.

Similar Species: Carolina Satyr (*page 207*) is similar, but is readily separated from Gemmed Satyr by its numerous eyespots on the underside of both wings.

Remarks: This species has a reddish wash on the upperside that can often be detected in flight.

Satyrs—Subfamily Satyrinae

Carolina Satyr *Hermeuptychia sosybius*

The underside has several cream-ringed, black submarginal eyespots and two dark median lines on both wings. For most of the year, the eyespots are large and obvious, but some emergences produce poorly marked individuals. The upperside is brown and unmarked. Wingspan: 1.25–1.5 in.

When and Where: Abundant but local year-round. A butterfly of shady woodlands, it sometimes ventures into more open areas such as roadsides, trails, and gardens. Often abundant, there is never a time when at least a few cannot be found. Larval foodplants are limited to grasses.

Similar Species: Gemmed Satyr (*page 206*) is similar on the upperside, but its underside lacks the numerous eyespots.

Remarks: The varied patterns of Carolina Satyrs have not been adequately explained.

Clearwings—Subfamily Ithomiinae

These are medium-sized, long-winged butterflies that generally lack wing scales, making the wings mostly transparent. Only one species has been recorded in the LRGV.

Klug's Clearwing *Dircenna klugii*

LRGV specialty. The long forewing and much shorter and rounded hindwing are transparent except for thin reddish veins. The abdomen is brown with white spots. The wings are tinted brown on females. Wingspan: 3–3.25 in.

When and Where: Accidental, with very old records (1877, 1902) for Cameron County only, in April. It is unlikely to occur again. Larval foodplants are members of the Solanaceae family.

Similar Species: There are no similar species in the United States.

Remarks: Several other clearwings occur in nearby Mexico; Klug's Clearwing, sometimes referred to as Klug's Dircenna, is known from Tamaulipas, San Luis Potosi, and Veracruz.

Monarchs—Subfamily Danainae

These large, orange-and-black butterflies utilize milkweeds as food-plants and nectar sources. The toxic chemicals they absorb from these plants make them distasteful to predators, providing vital protection. Sexes are easily determined by the large black pheromone scale on the interior edge of the male's hindwing, absent on the female. Flight shows a flapping and gliding pattern.

Monarch *Danaus plexippus*

One of the best known of all North American butterflies, it is easily identified by its large size and orange color with black veins and wide black margins sprinkled with tiny white spots. The underside has yellow-orange "windows" between the black veins. Wingspan: 3.5–4.75 in.

When and Where: Widespread and common year-round. Although it has been recorded every month, it is most numerous during migrations, from February to April and from November to December. The majority of sightings are of passing individuals in flight, but they often stop to feed on flowering plants.

Similar Species: Viceroy (*page 166*) is most alike, but it has a postmedian line on the hindwings that is black or black broken by white spots. Queen (*page 212*) is similar but is smaller, with a solid orange-brown color that lacks the heavy black veins on the upperside. **Soldier** (*page 214*) is also similar but lacks the heavy black veins on the upperside and the large yellow-orange windows on the underside.

Remarks: Monarchs migrate in spring and fall, although no individual butterfly makes the entire round-trip journey.

Queen *Danaus gilippus*

The upperside is deep orange-brown with numerous white spots on the forewing—including two white spots on the submarginal area of the inner forewing—and black margins with tiny white spots. The underside of the hindwing has a network of black veins; the forewing duplicates the upperside by not having obvious veins. Wingspan: 2.75–3.75 in.

Monarch and Queen

When and Where: Widespread and abundant year-round. One of the most abundant of the larger Valley butterflies, Queens can be found almost anywhere there are flowering plants. They are most numerous in fall when immigrants from the north join with local residents. They often converge at gardens.

Similar Species: Monarch (*page 210*) is most often mistaken for a Queen, but it has heavy black veins on the upperside. **Soldier** (*page 214*) is most alike and is separated from the Queen by the absence of the two white spots on the submarginal area of the inner forewing. Viceroy (*page 166*) is also similar but has heavy black veins on the upperside and a postmedian line on the hindwings that is black or black broken by white spots.

Remarks: Adults regularly roost communally, and this species is one of the earliest to fly in the mornings.

Monarchs—Subfamily Danainae

Soldier *Danaus eresimus*

LRGV specialty. The upperside is very much like the Queen—deep orange-brown with numerous white spots on the forewing. The Soldier lacks the two white spots on the submarginal area of the inner forewing. The underside is similar but with white edges on several of the black hindwing veins. Wingspan: 2.5–3.5 in.

When and Where: Widespread but uncommon, from April to January. It is never abundant, but it occurs somewhat regularly at flowering plants, especially in gardens.

Similar Species: Queen (*page 212*) is most alike but has two white spots on the submarginal area of the inner forewing. Monarch (*page 210*) and Viceroy (*page 166*) are also similar. Both have heavy black veins on the upperside. The Viceroy also has a postmedian line on the hindwings that is black or black broken by white spots.

Remarks: The Soldier is probably more common than reported because of its similarity to the abundant Queen.

Skippers—Family Hesperiidae

Skippers comprise an extremely diverse group of tiny to large butter-flies that can be black, brown, gray, yellow, or orange in color. Both sexes have well-developed walking legs. The tip of each antennae is bent downward in a thick and flattened extension (apiculus), rather than being knobbed, as it typically is in other butterflies.

Most species have large eyes and hairy bodies. They are generally strong fliers, and their flight pattern is usually jerky or "skipping," pro-viding them with their common name.

Those in the LRGV fall into four subfamilies: Spread-wing Skippers, Skipperlings (or Intermediate Skippers), Grass-Skippers (or Closed-wing Skippers), and Giant-Skippers.

Spread-wing Skippers—Subfamily Pyrginae

Adults typically rest with their wings spread, providing the observer an excellent view of their upperside, but some longtails and a few other spread-wing skippers perch with closed wings. Males never have a stigma but often have a costal fold.

Beautiful Beamer *Phocides belus*

LRGV specialty. The upperside is shiny black with blue-green streaks on the body and basal portion of the forewing. There are large clear "windows" on the forewing and blue-green bands and spots on the hindwing. The underside is similar. Wingspan: 2–2.75 in.

When and Where: Accidental, with a single April 2003 record of this species. (See the 2003 article by Hanson, Knudson, and Bordelon, listed in Appendix 2, References.) It does occur in nearby Mexico, so additional sightings are possible.

Similar Species: **Guava Skipper** (*page 218*) is most alike but lacks the large clear "windows" on the forewings; its blue-green bands are less extensive. The very similar Rainbow Skipper (*Phocides urania*) (*page 335*) resides in nearby Mexico and should be looked for; it has narrower "windows" on the forewing and less streaking on the body.

Remarks: The butterfly in the representative photo is the first U. S. record for this species, discovered and photographed by Dave Hanson.

Guava Skipper *Phocides polybius*

LRGV specialty. A gorgeous, shiny-black skipper with blue-green body and basal stripes on the upperside. It has a two-spot red bar on the leading edge of the forewing, a narrow golden collar, and white fringes. The underside is black with white fringes, and the golden throat is visible. Flight is swift and direct, although it has a tendency when feeding to fly out and circle before alighting again. Wingspan: 2–2.75 in.

When and Where: Widespread but uncommon year-round, more common in the fall. Never found in numbers, they often feed at wild olive flowers. This skipper is most active in the mornings and late afternoons. Larval foodplants are limited to guavas.

Similar Species: No other regularly occurring skipper in the LRGV is similar. There is, however, a lone record of the closely related **Beautiful Beamer** (*page 217*). It is also streaked with blue-green, but it has large, clear "windows" on the forewing.

Remarks: Larvae feed at night and live in leaf nests. Plantings of ornamental guava plants apparently have increased the numbers of this lovely skipper in recent years.

Spread-wing Skippers—Subfamily Pyrginae

Mercurial Skipper *Proteides mercurius*

LRGV specialty. A skipper that is well-marked on the upperside, with a gold head and wing base. The long, narrow forewing is reddish-brown with a median band of four white spots. The hindwing has a short tail-lobe. Fresh adults have a white hindwing fringe. The underside is two-toned, with a chestnut-brown basal area and gray outer half. Wingspan: 2.5–2.75 in.

When and Where: Rare, recorded in April and October. The majority of reports are from gardens. Larval foodplants consist of members of the legume family, including cassias and savi.

Similar Species: Broken Silverdrop (*page 220*) also has a gold head, but its underside is rusty with a silver patch on the hindwing.

Remarks: Larvae live in leaf nests.

Spread-wing Skippers—Subfamily Pyrginae

Broken Silverdrop *Epargyreus exadeus*

LRGV specialty. This skipper has a gold head and long rusty forewings. The rusty underside has a silver patch and thin silver streaks on the hindwing, as well as a wide gray margin. The upperside is dark brown with a median band of silver spots. Wingspan: 1.75–2.5 in.

When and Where: Accidental, recorded only in October. It resides in nearby Mexico, so additional sightings are possible. It is most likely to be found in gardens feeding on flowering plants. Larval food-plants consist of legumes, including cassias, beans, and sennas.

Similar Species: No other LRGV skipper has a bright silver patch on the underside of the hindwing and a long chestnut forewing. The similar Silver-spotted Skipper (*page 335*) does not reach the LRGV.

Remarks: This skipper may be more than a rare stray; recent sightings suggest it may be a rare resident.

Hammock Skipper *Polygonus leo*

The underside of the hindwing has two black median bands and a small black basal spot near the leading edge. Fresh individuals have a violet sheen in the right light. The upperside is dark brown to black, paler at the base, with three large, silver median squares and three tiny subapical spots on the forewing. It has a short tail-lobe on the hindwing. Wingspan: 1.75–2.5 in.

When and Where: Accidental, in March, April, and from September to November. It does occur in nearby Mexico, so additional sightings are possible. It is most likely to be found in gardens, especially those near the floodplain. There are no known local larval foodplants.

Similar Species: Dingy Purplewing (*page 173*) and Florida Purplewing (*page 174*) are somewhat alike, but purplewings have rounded hindwings and lack the skipper's bent apiculus. Manuel's Skipper (*page 222*), with historical records only, is similar but has reddish areas on the underside of the hindwing.

Remarks: Some authors call this "Violet Skipper." Strays have been recorded from south Texas west to southern California.

Manuel's Skipper *Polygonus manueli*

The underside of the hindwing is brown with a "powdery, bluish" basal gloss and two dark median bands, edged with reddish scales. A slight tail-lobe is also present. The forewing has three large, pearly-white center squares and three small subapical spots. The upperside of the hindwing is dark brown with a darker margin; the forewing is similar to the underside. Wingspan: 1.5–1.75 in.

When and Where: Historical only, recorded from August to October. Since it occurs in nearby Mexico, additional sightings are possible. Pyle reports that it "often perches among foliage with its wings closed, making it difficult to spot." Larval foodplants include shrubs of the legume family.

Similar Species: Hammock Skipper (*page 221*) is similar but is larger and lacks the reddish areas on the hindwing.

Remarks: This species, sometimes known as "Tidal Skipper" due to its affinity for coastal areas, also occurs in south Florida.

Spread-wing Skippers—Subfamily Pyrginae

White-striped Longtail *Chioides catillus*

The well-marked underside of this long-tailed skipper has a broad snow-white stripe that diagonally crosses the dark-brown hindwing. It also has a black wedge near the tip of the square forewing. The upperside, although not often seen, has several large, pale-yellow median squares and a line of subapical spots. Wingspan: 1.75–2 in.

When and Where: Widespread but uncommon year-round. It feeds on a wide variety of flowering plants along roadsides and in gardens. Larval foodplants include several vine-like members of the legume family, such as beans and peas.

Similar Species: Although there are several other long-tailed skippers (*pages 224–241*) found in the LRGV, none has such a distinct underwing pattern.

Remarks: This is a tropical species with a range that extends northward into southeastern Arizona, south Texas, and along the Texas Gulf Coast.

Zilpa Longtail *Chioides zilpa*

LRGV specialty. The underside is mottled black and brown with a large whitish patch on the inner edge of the hindwing and a black wedge near the tip of the square forewing. The upperside is dark brown with large, pale-yellow median patches and a short line of subapical spots. Wingspan: 2–2.5 in.

When and Where: Widespread but occasional, from March to April and September to November, when it's slightly more common. It is most likely to be found at flowering shrubs. Larval foodplants include legume vines, such as nissolia.

Similar Species: **White-crescent Longtail** (*page 231*) is most alike but lacks the square wingtips and black apical wedge. It also has a shorter tail. White-striped Longtail (*page 223*) is also similar, but its white underside stripe is far more extensive.

Remarks: Sightings of this tropical species have increased substantially in recent years. It is known to wander widely and has been recorded north to Kansas and west to Arizona.

Spread-wing Skippers—Subfamily Pyrginae

Gold-spotted Aguna *Aguna asander*

LRGV specialty. The underside is brown, often with a golden hue or sometimes a purplish sheen, and has a broad white median band and a tail-like lobe. The upperside has a broad median band of gold squares across the long, narrow, golden-brown forewing. The hindwing is slightly scalloped and has a very short tail-lobe. Wingspan: 2–2.25 in.

When and Where: Rare, from April to January. It is most likely at gardens near wooded areas, often in the vicinity of orchid trees, its larval foodplant.

Similar Species: **Tailed Aguna** (*page 227*) and **White-crescent Longtail** (*page 231*) also have a gold-banded forewing on the upperside, but both have a longer tail. **Emerald Aguna** (*page 226*) is similar in shape and pattern but has a green body and wing base.

Remarks: Adults often perch under leaves.

Emerald Aguna *Aguna claxon*

LRGV specialty. The body and the wing base are bright emerald green. The underside of the dark-brown hindwing has a silver-white median band and a tail-like lobe. The upperside has a median forewing band of yellow squares. Wingspan: 1.5–1.75 in.

When and Where: Rare, recorded only in January, October, and November. It is most likely to be found at flowering shrubs in gardens, especially near orchid trees, its larval foodplant. Recent (2002) records come from Weslaco.

Similar Species: **Tailed Aguna** (*page 227*), Long-tailed Skipper (*page 232*), and **Esmeralda Longtail** (*page 235*) have green backs but also have long tails. **Gold-spotted Aguna** (*page 225*) has a similar pattern, including a tail-like lobe, but lacks the green body and wing base. No other "tailless" skipper has a green back.

Remarks: On the infrequent occasions when it was found before 2002, it was considered an accidental stray.

Tailed Aguna *Aguna metophis*

LRGV specialty. The underside is dark brown with a paler base and a narrow white median band on the hindwing, a pale-brown marginal patch on the forewing, and a moderately long tail. The upperside shows a dull-greenish body and wing base. The brown forewing has a median band of yellowish squares, a lone tiny center spot, and a sub-apical line of tiny yellowish spots. Wingspan: 1.75–2 in.

When and Where: Occasional, from August to January. Most records are from gardens in the vicinity of orchid trees, its larval foodplant.

Similar Species: Long-tailed Skipper (*page 232*) and **Esmeralda Longtail** (*page 235*) also have a green back and long tails, but neither has a whitish median band on the underside. **Gold-spotted Aguna** (*page 225*) has a white median band on the underside but lacks the dull-green back and long tails.

Remarks: Records of this tropical aguna have increased in recent years.

Mottled Longtail *Typhedanus undulatus*

LRGV specialty. The black-and-brown underside is strongly mottled and has a pale outer hindwing margin and a wide black tail. The upperside is brown with large, glassy, white median spots and a faint subapical line. Wingspan: 1.5–1.75 in.

When and Where: Accidental, with historical records only from August to November. Larval foodplants include cassias.

Similar Species: No other longtail has a similar underside pattern.

Remarks: This is a species of more arid habitats, so it is most likely to occur in the drier, western portion of the LRGV.

Spread-wing Skippers—Subfamily Pyrginae

Mexican Longtail *Polythrix mexicanus*

LRGV specialty. The upperside of the forewing has three large, glassy median spots, two dark spots on the inner margin, and a line of sub-apical spots. The hindwing is marked with a few dark spots and bands. The underside is similar but with a dark spot on the forewing. The tails are long and narrow with darker tips (not shown on the worn individual in the photograph below). Wingspan: 1.5–1.75 in.

When and Where: Accidental, in July and October. Because it occurs in nearby Mexico, additional sightings are possible. Larval foodplants include various legumes.

Similar Species: **Eight-spotted Longtail** (*page 230*) is most alike but lacks the two dark spots on the inner margin of the forewing's upperside. Its tails are much shorter.

Remarks: This species often perches beneath leaves.

Eight-spotted Longtail *Polythrix octomaculata*

LRGV specialty. This longtail is dark brown on the upperside with a band of glassy whitish squares near the leading edge and three sub-apical spots on the forewing. The underside is similar in males, but some females have a whitish median patch on the hindwing. The tails are relatively short; those of males are shorter than those of females. Wingspan: 1.5–1.75 in.

When and Where: Accidental, in March, September, and October. It is relatively common in nearby Mexico, so additional sightings are possible. Larval foodplants include various legumes found south of the border.

Similar Species: **Mexican Longtail** (*page 229*) is most alike but is paler with three large, glassy median spots and two dark spots on the inner margin of the forewing. Its tails are longer.

Remarks: The Polythrix skippers perch with wings spread.

Spread-wing Skippers—Subfamily Pyrginae

White-crescent Longtail *Codatractus alcaeus*

LRGV specialty. The underside is strongly marked with an elongated white submarginal patch (edged inside with black) and two additional broad black bands. The upperside is brown with a median band of gold spots, a central spot, and a curved subapical line on the forewing; the hindwing is unmarked. The margins are checkered, and the tails are narrow and moderately long. Wingspan: 1.75–2.25 in.

When and Where: Accidental, recorded only in October. It resides in nearby Mexico, so additional sightings are possible. Larval food-plants include tree legume species, none of which occur in the LRGV.

Similar Species: **Zilpa Longtail** (*page 224*) is most alike, with its white underwing patch and black forewing spots, but it has a black wedge near the square wingtip.

Remarks: Worn individuals can easily be confused with other long-tails, unless seen extremely well.

Spread-wing Skippers—Subfamily Pyrginae

Long-tailed Skipper *Urbanus proteus*

This longtail is best identified from the upperside by its greenish back, yellowish forewing spots that form an arc, and checkered margins. The underside of the hindwing is brown with a broad, unbroken, black submarginal band and four black basal spots. The tail can be extremely long. Wingspan: 1.5–2.25 in.

When and Where: Widespread but uncommon year-round. It can usually be found at flowering plants along roadsides and in gardens. Larval foodplants consist of several legumes, including beans.

Similar Species: There are several other green-bodied, long-tailed skippers. **Tailed Aguna** (*page 227*) is somewhat alike but has a white-striped underside. **Pronus Longtail** (*page 233*) has a blue-green abdomen, but the color does not extend onto the back. **Double-striped Longtail** (*page 234*) has two unbroken bands on the underside of the hindwing. **Esmeralda Longtail** (*page 235*) has a green back, but the green extends across much of the hindwing.

Remarks: This is the most widespread of the Texas longtails. Its range extends throughout much of the Southeast and northward into the mid-Atlantic states. Larvae live in rolled or tied leaves.

Pronus Longtail *Urbanus pronus*

LRGV specialty. The upperside has a blue-green abdomen and hind-wing base; the color does not extend onto the back. The dark-brown forewing has a median band of silvery squares, a lone central spot, and a short subapical bar. The dark tail is relatively short. The underside of the hindwing has several dark spots that form a broad post-median band and an inner band with two separate spots near the leading edge. Wingspan: 1.5–1.75 in.

When and Where: Accidental, recorded only once in October. Since it does occur in nearby Mexico, additional sightings are possible. Larval foodplants are unknown.

Similar Species: **Esmeralda Longtail** (*page 235*) and several other long-tails have a greenish body (see the discussion in the Long-tailed Skipper account, page 232), but only in the Pronus Longtail does the blue-green abdomen color not extend onto the back.

Remarks: Neck refers to this species as "Short-tailed Green Longtail."

Double-striped Longtail *Urbanus belli*

LRGV specialty. The upperside shows this longtail's green body, and the forewing has a median band of large square patches and a pair of subapical spots. The hindwing is unmarked except for a scalloped white margin, and the tails are broad but relatively short. The underside of the forewing is similar, but the hindwing has two broad, unbroken, black bands. Wingspan: 1.5–1.75 in.

When and Where: Historical only, there is a lone, June 1968 record from Brownsville. However, it is "the most frequently encountered green-bodied Urbanus species in most of Mexico," according to Warren (1997), so additional records are possible.

Similar Species: Long-tailed Skipper (*page 232*) and **Pronus** (*page 233*) and **Esmeralda** (*page 235*) **longtails** are also green-bodied, but only the Double-striped Longtail has two unbroken bands on the underside of the hindwing. Field identification of all these green-bodied longtails is difficult.

Remarks: Fresh individuals have a noticeable checkered fringe on the forewing.

Esmeralda Longtail *Urbanus esmeraldus*

LRGV specialty. Fresh individuals exhibit more green on the back, abdomen, and upperside of the hindwings than any of the other LRGV longtails. The dark-brown forewing has a median band of silvery squares, a lone central spot, and a short subapical line of tiny white spots. Males have a noticeable costal fold. The underside of the hindwing has two dark bands, including a short outer band and an extended central band. There are also four dark basal spots. Wingspan: 1.25–1.5 in.

When and Where: Accidental, recorded only in August. It occurs in nearby Mexico, so additional sightings are possible. Larval foodplants include beggar's tick and tickclover.

Similar Species: **Pronus Longtail** (*page 233*) is most alike but lacks a green back and has a shorter tail. Long-tailed Skipper (*page 232*) is similar, due to the extensive green color on the back, but the color barely extends onto the wings. **Double-striped Longtail** (*page 234*) has two unbroken bands on the underside of the hindwing.

Remarks: This is one of the least known of the LRGV longtails.

Dorantes Longtail *Urbanus dorantes*

The underside of fresh individuals has a lavender sheen on the hindwing with two broad, broken, dark median bands and a single basal spot. The forewing has a pale bar on the leading edge and a dark submarginal band that is divided by a pale area just below the wingtip. The upperside of the forewing is brown with four translucent, yellowish squares and a short subapical line. Wingspan: 1.5–2 in.

When and Where: Widespread but uncommon year-round. It frequents flowering plants along roadsides and in gardens. Larval foodplants include a variety of legumes.

Similar Species: No other longtail exhibits a lavender sheen and a divided dark submarginal band on the underside of the forewing.

Remarks: This longtail was once known as "Lilac-banded Longtail" because of the lavender sheen, which disappears with age.

Spread-wing Skippers—Subfamily Pyrginae

Teleus Longtail *Urbanus teleus*

LRGV specialty. The upperside has two straight white bands across the brown forewing. The inner band is unbroken and extends almost to the trailing edge; the much shorter subapical band is composed of four white spots. The underside shows white margins and has two dark bands on the otherwise brown hindwings; the outer band is fairly even on its inner edge. Wingspan: 1.5–1.75 in.

When and Where: Rare, from May to January. It is most likely to be found at flowering plants in gardens. Larval foodplants are limited to grasses.

Similar Species: **Tanna Longtail** (*page 238*) is nearly identical, but the longer forewing line is crooked and broken. Its subapical band has five or more spots, instead of four. The common **Brown Longtail** (*page 240*) is also alike. Although male Browns lack the white wing bands, some females have wing bands that can be as white as those of Teleus. Female Browns can best be separated from Teleus by the underside of the Brown's hindwing, which lacks the white margin and has a narrower, dark outer band.

Remarks: This species is easily mistaken for the far more common Brown Longtail. Young larvae make a nest in a folded blade of grass.

Tanna Longtail *Urbanus tanna*

LRGV specialty. This species, almost identical to **Teleus Longtail** (*page 237*), has a dark-brown forewing with two narrow, white bands—a long, slightly crooked inner one and a short subapical band with five or more spots. The hindwing has a pale fringe. The underside has two dark bands on the hindwing, a full outer band and a short inner band. There are two dark spots near the leading edge. Wingspan: 1.25–1.5 in.

When and Where: Accidental, in June and December. It occurs in nearby Mexico, so additional sightings are possible. Larval food-plants are unknown.

Similar Species: Teleus Longtail (*page 237*) is most alike, but the inner forewing line is straight and unbroken, and the subapical area has four, rather than five, spots.

Remarks: Because of its close similarity to Teleus Longtail, Tanna Longtail may go undetected.

Spread-wing Skippers—Subfamily Pyrginae

Plain Longtail *Urbanus simplicius*

LRGV specialty. True to its name, the Plain Longtail is generally unmarked on the upperside, although faint median and subapical lines do occur on the forewing. The underside has two faint, but broad and unbroken, darker bands on the hindwing. Wingspan: 1.5–2 in.

When and Where: Accidental, recorded only in April. Since this species does occur in nearby Mexico, additional sightings are possible. Larval foodplants include vine-like legumes, such as beans.

Similar Species: **Brown Longtail** (*page 240*) is very similar, but the Brown's underside inner hindwing band is broken. Female Browns may have whitish forewing bands, never present on Plain Longtails.

Remarks: Because of its similarity to Brown Longtail, it may be more common than the lone record suggests.

Brown Longtail *Urbanus procne*

LRGV specialty. Most individuals are all-brown on the upperside, but females may have one or two thin, whitish bands across the forewing. The underside of the hindwing has two broad, dark bands. The inner band is broken, and the outer unbroken band has a distinct notch or two on the upper portion of the inner edge. Wingspan: 1.5–1.75 in.

When and Where: Widespread and common year-round. The most numerous of the various longtails in the LRGV, it has been recorded at flowering plants almost everywhere. Larval foodplants consist of various grasses, including the common Bermudagrass and Johnsongrass.

Similar Species: The very rare **Plain Longtail** (*page 239*) is virtually identical but has two faint, unbroken dark bands on the underside of the hindwing. **Teleus Longtail** (*page 237*) can be similar to some female Brown Longtails, but the forewing bands are straight and wider. The dark outer band on the underside of the Brown's hindwing is narrower, and Teleus usually has white hindwing margins.

Remarks: Brown and Teleus longtails are the only known North American longtails that utilize grasses as their larval foodplants. Young larvae live in nests made from folded leaf tips.

Spread-wing Skippers—Subfamily Pyrginae

White-tailed Longtail *Urbanus doryssus*

LRGV specialty. The White-tailed is very unlike the other LRGV longtails. The upperside of the hindwing is dark brown with bright-white margins and short tails. Female forewings are unmarked, but males have a broken white median band and a short three-spot subapical line. The underside is brown with a broad white hindwing margin. Wingspan: 1.25–1.75 in.

When and Where: Accidental, from March to July and in October and November. Present in nearby Mexico, so additional sightings are possible. Larval foodplants include various legumes.

Similar Species: The contrasting dark wings and white tail are unique to the LRGV skippers.

Remarks: This tropical skipper ranges south as far as Argentina. Its rapid flight prompted Pyle to write that it gives "the impression of a flying streak."

Spread-wing Skippers—Subfamily Pyrginae

Two-barred Flasher *Astraptes fulgerator*

LRGV specialty. The Two-barred Flasher is a striking spread-wing skipper with a turquoise-blue back and forewing base and two white forewing bands. The inner band is broad and broken; the subapical band consists of four spots. The underside is black with white on the leading edge of the hindwing. The head and thorax are yellow. Wingspan: 2–2.5 in.

When and Where: Widespread but occasional and somewhat sporadic. Records exist for every month but February. Present in good numbers some years, but rare or absent others. Most sightings are at flowering shrubs. The larval foodplant is coyotillo.

Similar Species: Only **Small-spotted Flasher** (*page 243*) has the same combination of colors, but it is smaller. Its median band is very narrow, and the subapical spots are barely noticeable. **Frosted Flasher** (*page 244*) is similar but lacks a white median band on the forewing. The similar but smaller **Gilbert's Flasher** (*page 245*) also lacks a white median band and is deep blue.

Remarks: This gorgeous skipper is known to some authors as "Blue Flasher" or "Flashing Astraptes." When feeding, it is often sufficiently docile to be photographed.

Small-spotted Flasher *Astraptes egregius*

LRGV specialty. The upperside is dark brown with a deep-blue-green body and wing base. The forewing is marked by a narrow median line of white spots, including a faint line on the leading edge, and tiny subapical spots. The hindwing has a short tail-like lobe. The underside is dark brown with a narrow yellow costal margin. Wingspan: 1.5–1.75 in.

When and Where: Accidental, recorded only in October. It occurs in nearby Mexico, so additional sightings are possible. Larval foodplants are unknown.

Similar Species: **Gilbert's Flasher** (*page 245*) is most alike but lacks a median forewing line. **Two-barred** (*page 242*) and **Frosted** (*page 244*) **flashers** are larger. Two-barred has a broad median band on the forewing, and Frosted has a turquoise back and basal area and a broad frosted margin on the underside of the hindwing.

Remarks: Several authors refer to this skipper as "Green Flasher."

Frosted Flasher *Astraptes alardus*

LRGV specialty. The Frosted Flasher has a turquoise body and basal area extending onto the wings, a long, narrow, unmarked, blackish-brown forewing, and a short tail-like lobe on the hindwing. Fresh individuals have a narrow whitish fringe on the brown hindwing. The brown underside has a broad frosted hindwing margin and white fringe. Wingspan: 2–2.5 in.

When and Where: Accidental, in June, September, and October. It is relatively common in nearby Mexico, so additional sightings are possible. Larval foodplants include coralbean.

Similar Species: **Two-barred Flasher** (*page 242*) is similar, but it has a broad white median band. **Small-spotted Flasher** (*page 243*) is smaller and has a narrow broken median band on the forewing. **Gilbert's Flasher** (*page 245*) is smaller and deep blue, rather than turquoise, on the body and basal area. It lacks the frosted margin on the underside of the hindwing.

Remarks: Neck refers to this species as "White Flasher," after the frosted underwing margin. Adults often rest under leaves.

Spread-wing Skippers—Subfamily Pyrginae

Gilbert's Flasher *Astraptes gilberti*

LRGV specialty. The upperside is dark brown and unmarked, except for an iridescent deep-blue body and basal area. The underside of the hindwing is brown with a dark median band and a white basal patch on the inner margin. Wingspan: 1.5–2 in.

When and Where: Accidental, recorded only in March and October. It is fairly common in nearby Mexico, so additional sightings are possible. Larval foodplants include orchid trees.

Similar Species: Frosted Flasher (*page 244*) is most alike but is larger, with a turquoise, instead of deep-blue, body and wing base and a frosted margin on the underside of the hindwing. The similar **Small-spotted Flasher** (*page 243*) has a broken white median line on the upperside forewing. The larger **Two-barred Flasher** (*page 242*) has two white forewing bars on the upperside.

Remarks: The common and scientific names for this species vary. Common names include Gilbert's Flasher, Hopffer's Flasher, and Mad Flasher.

Yellow-tipped Flasher *Astraptes anaphus*

LRGV specialty. The upperside is dark brown with faint dark bands and yellow hindwing lobes. The underside is rusty-brown with two faint, brown bands. The outer edges of the hindwing and lobe are bright yellow. Wingspan: 2–2.5 in.

When and Where: Rare, recorded in April and from September to November. It is relatively common in nearby Mexico, so additional sightings are possible. Larval foodplants include various vine-like legumes, such as beans.

Similar Species: No other LRGV skipper is marked with yellow lobes on the hindwings.

Remarks: Because of its rather plain upperside (with the exception of the yellow hindwing lobes), some authors refer to this species as "Yellow Flasher" or "Dull Astraptes."

Coyote Cloudywing *Achalarus toxeus*

This rather plain brown skipper appears to have little more than a white hindwing fringe, but a closer look at the upperside will reveal a series of pale median patches on the forewing. On worn individuals, these marks can look like scratches, and the white fringes can be difficult to discern. The underside is brown with two faint, dark bands and white fringe on the rounded hindwing. Wingspan: 1.5–2 in.

When and Where: Widespread but uncommon year-round. Most sightings are at flowering plants, especially in gardens. Larval foodplants include Texas ebony and blackbrush acacia.

Similar Species: The very similar **Jalapus Cloudywing** (*page 248*) has also been recorded in the LRGV a few times. It is identical except that the hindwing has an extended lobe.

Remarks: Coyote Cloudywings are most active early and late in the day. Once considered a rare stray in the United States, it is more numerous farther north in DeWitt and Victoria counties.

Jalapus Cloudywing *Achalarus jalapus*

LRGV specialty. The upperside is dark brown with a series of pale median patches on the forewing. The hindwing has a white fringe and tail lobe. The underside of the hindwing has two faint, dark bands and a white fringe. Wingspan: 1.5–1.75 in.

When and Where: Accidental, from July to November. It is also rare in nearby Mexico, but additional sightings are possible. Larval food-plants are unknown.

Similar Species: Coyote Cloudywing (*page 247*) is identical except that it lacks the hindwing lobe.

Remarks: Some authors place this species in the genus Thessia.

Northern Cloudywing *Thorybes pylades*

The upperside is dark brown with a series of small, unaligned, transparent forewing spots, as well as a subapical line, unmarked hindwings, and checkered brown fringes. The underside is brown with two short, gray bars on the leading edge of the forewing. Wingspan: 1.25–1.75 in.

When and Where: Accidental, probably a stray from the north in spring. Larval foodplants include a variety of legumes, such as beans and vetches.

Similar Species: Two somewhat similar LRGV duskywings—Mournful (*page 279*) and Funereal (*page 280*)—have white fringes on the trailing edge of the hindwings.

Remarks: The range of this cloudywing extends throughout much of the East, the Rocky Mountain states, and most of Mexico, barely touching the western portion of the LRGV.

Potrillo Skipper *Cabares potrillo*

LRGV specialty. The upperside of this pale-brown skipper shows a median band of square glassy spots across the forewing (one spot is saddle-shaped) and a much shorter subapical band. The seldom-seen underside is pale brown with two dark median bands and a dark wingtip. Wingspan: 1-1.5 in.

When and Where: Uncommon, from April to February. Some years it can be more numerous. It frequents flowering plants along roadsides and in gardens. Larval foodplants are limited to Barbadoscherry.

Similar Species: Only the very rare **Stallings' Flat** (*page 252*), with a wider spot-band, is similar. It lacks the saddle-shaped forewing spot.

Remarks: The saddle-shaped forewing spot has also been described as a sideways U.

Spread-wing Skippers—Subfamily Pyrginae

Fritzgaertner's Flat *Celaenorrhinus fritzgaertneri*

LRGV specialty. The upperside of the forewing is gray-brown with an uneven median band of large white spots, three white subapical spots, and a lone white basal spot edged with black. The hindwing is mottled and has a checkered fringe. The underside of the hindwing is also mottled; the forewing is identical to the upperside. Wingspan: 1.5–1.75 in.

When and Where: Accidental, in February, July, September, and November. Since it is relatively common in nearby Mexico, additional sightings are possible. It sometimes feeds at flowering plants at dawn. Larval foodplants include members of the Acanthaceae family.

Similar Species: **Stallings' Flat** (*page 252*) is most alike but is brown instead of gray-brown. Its hindwing fringe is not checkered.

Remarks: The flats are considered crepuscular, principally active at dawn and dusk. They often perch under leaves or in sheltered places during midday.

Stallings' Flat *Celaenorrhinus stallingsi*

LRGV specialty. Mottled brown on the upperside, it has a median band of large white squares and three small subapical spots on the forewing. The rounded hindwing is brown with a darker center. The underside is similar. Wingspan: 1.25–1.75 in.

When and Where: Very rare, in June, August, and from October to December. Resident in nearby Mexico, so additional sightings are possible. Most active at dawn and dusk, it perches on the ground or on solid objects such as culverts. Larval foodplants are unknown in the LRGV, but it utilizes members of the Acanthaceae family in adjacent Mexico.

Similar Species: **Fritzgaertner's Flat** (*page 251*) is most alike but is gray-brown with noticeably checkered hindwing fringes. **Potrillo Skipper** (*page 250*) has similar colors, but the narrower forewing median band includes a saddle-shaped spot.

Remarks: The status of this species is uncertain in the LRGV; it may be accidental only.

Falcate Skipper *Spathilepia clonius*

LRGV specialty. The upperside is blackish with a broad median band of snow-white squares, a line of tiny subapical spots near the square wingtips, and scalloped margins. The underside is also dark with a large, triangular, black patch on the leading edge of the hindwing and a broad white median band on the forewing. In the right light, the underside can appear bluish. It often perches with wings partially open. Wingspan: 1.5–1.75 in.

When and Where: Rare, from May to July and October to December. It frequents flowering plants throughout. Larval foodplants include various legumes, such as beans and peas.

Similar Species: It is the only blackish skipper in the LRGV with a broad white median band on the upperside. The similar **Stallings' Flat** (*page 252*) is pale brown.

Remarks: This is a powerful skipper with a fast flight. Males often perch on high foliage awaiting females.

Spread-wing Skippers—Subfamily Pyrginae

Mimosa Skipper *Cogia calchas*

LRGV specialty. Mimosa Skippers usually perch with closed wings. The underside is mottled brown with a lavender-gray wash on the base and center of the hindwing. There are whitish patches near the wingtip and on the leading edge of the forewing. The upperside is brown with three or four tiny subapical spots. Wingspan: 1.25–1.75 in.

When and Where: Widespread and common year-round. It frequents a diversity of habitats, from moist areas to drier woodlands, as well as gardens. Larval foodplants are limited to black mimosa. It is most easily found at Santa Ana National Wildlife Refuge.

Similar Species: A perched individual could only be confused with a longtail missing its tail. The similar but very rare Acacia Skipper (*page 255*) has a whitish hindwing margin and an obviously checkered forewing fringe.

Remarks: The range of this tropical skipper extends only to the LRGV; it has not been recorded northward. Larvae live in rolled or tied leaves.

Acacia Skipper *Cogia hippalus*

Acacia Skippers usually perch with closed wings. The underside of the hindwing, which often has a purplish cast, has two broad, dark, jagged median bands and a wide frosted margin (with tiny black spots). There is a checkered fringe on the forewing. The upperside is brown with a median band of white spots, two tiny center spots, and tiny subapical spots. The hindwing has a pale fringe. Wingspan: 1.5-1.75 in.

When and Where: Accidental, in April, August, and September. It is most likely to be found at flowering shrubs along roadsides or in other open areas. Larval foodplants include fern acacia.

Similar Species: The Hoary Edge, Desert Cloudywing, and Arizona Skipper are similar but do not occur in the LRGV. Outis Skipper (*page 256*), similar but smaller, has probably been extirpated from south Texas. It has smaller forewing spots and lacks the frosted margin on the underside of the hindwing. **Mimosa Skipper** (*page 254*) lacks the frosted margin and checkered fringe.

Remarks: Acacia Skipper is a western species, found in the southern Trans-Pecos of Texas and west into central Arizona. Some authors refer to this species as "White-edged Skipper."

Spread-wing Skippers—Subfamily Pyrginae

Outis Skipper *Cogia outis*

The underside of the hindwing is brown with two broad, darker bands and checkered fringes. The upperside of the forewing is brown with a median line of transparent white spots and several white subapical spots. The hindwing has a single white basal spot. The antennae shaft is checkered. Wingspan: 1.25–1.75 in.

When and Where: Accidental, in April. Rare throughout its central Texas range, so additional sightings in the LRGV are unlikely. Larval foodplants include fern acacia.

Similar Species: Acacia Skipper (*page 255*) is most alike but is larger with bigger forewing spots and a frosted margin on the underside.

Remarks: Scott refers to this species as "Texas Acacia Skipper," and he also mentions that it flies with Acacia Skippers.

Starred Skipper *Arteurotia tractipennis*

LRGV specialty. The Starred Skipper is gray-brown on the upperside. The leading edge of the forewing has a large black patch—with three white spots on its outer edge—and two dark median bars. The leading half of the hindwing is dark. The underside is orange-brown with a whitish median patch on the hindwing. Wingspan: 1.25–1.5 in.

When and Where: Accidental, in September and November. Since it occurs in nearby Mexico, additional sightings are possible. Larval foodplants include crotons.

Similar Species: Only **Walker's Metalmark** (*page 114*) could possibly be confused with this skipper. It has a similar black forewing patch but has numerous dark spots forming a checkered pattern on the upperside.

Remarks: This is one of the many unexpected species recorded during the extraordinary 2003 fall season.

Purplish-black Skipper *Nisoniades rubescens*

LRGV specialty. A black and dark-brown skipper that can appear purplish in the right light. The upperside is darkest on the basal portion, with horizontal bands of brown on the rather squared hindwing. It has three tiny, white subapical spots on the pointed forewing. Males are darker than females. The underside is similar. Wingspan: 1–1.5 in.

When and Where: Accidental, recorded only in October and November. It occurs in nearby Mexico, so additional sightings are possible. Larval foodplants include morningglories.

Similar Species: **Glazed Pellicia** (*page 259*) is most alike but lacks the subapical spots and has a violet sheen in the right light.

Remarks: In nearby Mexico, it frequents a wide range of habitats from the tropical lowlands to oak woodlands at higher elevations.

Glazed Pellicia *Pellicia arina*

LRGV specialty. The upperside appears very dark, but in the right light, faint banding and an extensive violet sheen are obvious. The underside is similar. Wingtips are pointed. Wingspan: 1.25–1.5 in.

When and Where: Widespread but occasional most years, in April and from June to January. Some years it is more numerous. It is most likely to be found at flowering plants along roadsides and in gardens. Larval foodplants are unknown, but since the closely related Morning Glory Pellicia utilizes morningglories, Glazed Pellicia may also.

Similar Species: **Purplish-black Skipper** (*page 258*) has tiny white subapical spots on the forewing upperside and more obvious banding on the rather square hindwing upperside. It lacks the violet sheen. **Morning Glory Pellicia** (*page 260*) is much smaller, and the violet sheen is barely evident.

Remarks: This spread-wing skipper appears to be on the increase in the LRGV.

Spread-wing Skippers—Subfamily Pyrginae

Morning Glory Pellicia *Pellicia dimidiata*

LRGV specialty. Sexually dimorphic, the female's upperside is mottled brown with a series of postmedian and submarginal pale spots edged with dark brown on the hindwing and outer half of the forewing. The forewing has a pale violet sheen and two dark bars on the leading edge. Males are darker and poorly marked. The underside has a series of white submarginal spots on the trailing edge of the hindwing. Wingspan: .75–1.25 in.

When and Where: Accidental, recorded only in October. Since it occurs in nearby Mexico, additional sightings are possible. Larval food-plants include morningglories, thus its common name.

Similar Species: **Glazed Pellicia** (*page 259*), with an extensive violet sheen, and **Purplish-black Skipper** (*page 258*), with a purple sheen and white subapical spots on the forewing upperside, are most alike, but both are larger.

Remarks: The range of this tropical skipper extends southward to Argentina.

Red-studded Skipper *Noctuana stator*

LRGV specialty. The upperside forewing is dark brown with reddish mottling, including a red bar near the falcate wingtip, and two tiny white subapical spots. The hindwing has three red patches on the outer edge and a reddish submarginal area. The margins are scalloped. The underside is mottled black and brown with one tiny and two large white subapical spots. Wingspan: 1–1.5 in.

When and Where: Accidental, with a single October record. Since it does occur in nearby Mexico, additional sightings are possible. Larval foodplants are unknown.

Similar Species: No other black-and-brown-mottled, LRGV skipper is marked with reddish patches and bars.

Remarks: Almost nothing is known about this extremely rare species.

Mottled Bolla *Bolla clytius*

LRGV specialty. Sexually dimorphic, the male's upperside is dark brown to black with a gray-brown postmedian area on the forewing. Females are mottled pale- and dark-brown with a blackish central patch on the forewing. Both have two tiny, transparent, white subapical spots and a similar central forewing spot. The hindwing shape is somewhat square. The underside is similar. Wingspan: 1–1.25 in.

When and Where: Accidental, from June to November. It is relatively common in nearby Mexico, so additional sightings are possible. Larval foodplants are unknown, but the closely related Obscure Bolla (historical record only) probably utilizes tomato plants.

Similar Species: The slightly smaller **Obscure Bolla** (*page 263*) is so similar that it probably cannot be safely separated from Mottled in the field. The Obscure sometimes shows a few scattered, tiny, orange spots on the underside of the hindwing. There is only one historical record of the Obscure Bolla. **Mazans Scallopwing** (*page 265*) is also alike, but its hindwing is scalloped and its forewing square.

Remarks: This is one of ten Bolla species known in northern Mexico.

Spread-wing Skippers—Subfamily Pyrginae

Obscure Bolla *Bolla brennus*

LRGV specialty. The upperside is dark brown with obscure blackish bands across both hindwings. The forewing is slightly pointed. Females have small subapical spots. The underside is similar with scattered, tiny, orange spots, not always present. Wingspan: .75–1.25 in.

When and Where: Accidental, with only one historical record, in October. Since this species occurs in nearby Mexico, additional sightings are possible. Larval foodplants probably include members of the Solanaceae family, such as tomato plants.

Similar Species: **Mottled Bolla** (*page 262*) is essentially identical. It lacks the tiny orange spots on the underside, but they are not always present on the Obscure. Separating the two species accurately can probably only be done by examination of the genitalia. **Mazans Scallopwing** (*page 265*) is also similar but has squared forewings and scalloped hindwings.

Remarks: According to Howe, this species has also been reported from Arizona.

Spread-wing Skippers—Subfamily Pyrginae

Golden-headed Scallopwing *Staphylus ceos*

This little skipper has a noticeable golden head and golden palpi. The upperside is blackish-brown with two tiny, white subapical spots; the underside is unmarked. The scalloped fringes are barely evident. Wingspan: 1–1.25 in.

When and Where: Rare, from March to December. It is more common in the western portion of the LRGV but occasionally wanders to the lower Valley. It feeds on low-growing wildflowers and often perches on the ground. Larval foodplants include members of the goosefoot family.

Similar Species: Although there are no other golden-headed, spread-wing skippers in the LRGV, worn individuals without a golden head could be confused with the more common **Mazans Scallopwing** (*page 265*), but it has more obvious scalloped fringes on the hindwing and a weaker flight.

Remarks: The range of this tropical skipper extends westward along the Rio Grande to West Texas and beyond. Some authors refer to it as "Ceos Skipper," after its scientific species name.

Mazans Scallopwing *Staphylus mazans*

LRGV specialty. Sexually dimorphic, the upperside of males is predominantly blackish-brown, while females are brown with black bands. Both have two tiny, white subapical spots, broad square wingtips, and scalloped hindwings. The underside is similar. Wingspan: 1–1.25 in.

When and Where: Widespread and common year-round. It prefers shady edges, often resting on the ground, and it rarely feeds very high above the ground. Larval foodplants include members of the Chenopodiaceae family, such as lamb's-quarters and pigweed.

Similar Species: **Mottled Bolla** (*page 262*) is most alike but has pointed, rather than square, wingtips and lacks the scalloped margin. Common Sootywing (*page 290*) is somewhat alike, especially when worn, but lacks the scalloped margin and has numerous white submarginal spots on the forewing.

Remarks: Mazans is sometimes known as "Tropical Sootywing" or "Southern Scalloped Sootywing." The northern-ranging, very similar Hayhurst's Scallopwing (*page 335*) is considered hypothetical in the LRGV.

Variegated Skipper *Gorgythion begga*

LRGV specialty. A tiny, heavily variegated skipper with a violet sheen and numerous black markings, including a broad, oddly shaped median band on the forewing and parallel lines on the hindwing. It has two tiny subapical spots. The underside is brown and poorly marked. Wingspan: .75–1.25 in.

When and Where: Accidental, with records only for March and December. It is relatively common in nearby Mexico, so additional sightings are possible. Larval foodplants are unknown.

Similar Species: There are no other small LRGV skippers with such a variegated pattern and a violet sheen. Beware, however, that Variegated Skipper cannot be separated from Crab's Claw (*Gorgythion vox*), a Mexican species, without examination of the genitalia.

Remarks: This unexpected species, which had not been recorded in the LRGV for many years, was reported in December 2003.

Spread-wing Skippers—Subfamily Pyrginae

Blue-studded Skipper *Sostrata bifasciata*

LRGV specialty. The upperside has dark-brown forewings and paler hindwings, both with scattered iridescent-blue scales throughout. The forewing has a black patch near the base, a white central triangle, darker forewing margins, and four whitish subapical spots. Females are lighter brown with fewer blue scales. The underside is brown with dark bands. Wingspan: 1–1.25 in.

When and Where: Accidental, recorded only in October. It is fairly common in Mexico, so additional sightings are possible. Larval foodplants are unknown.

Similar Species: No other LRGV skipper has scattered blue flecks.

Remarks: In Mexico, this skipper prefers dry scrublands, habitat that is not regularly surveyed in the LRGV.

Spread-wing Skippers—Subfamily Pyrginae

Tropical Duskywing *Anastrus sempiternus*

LRGV specialty. The upperside is dark brown with numerous large, pale spots on the forewing and smaller pale spots near the pointed wingtips. The hindwing has a broad dark postmedian band, a line of pale submarginal spots, and a broad dark margin. The underside is similar, except the lower half of the hindwing is pale. Wingspan: 1.25–1.5 in.

When and Where: Accidental, with only two records, one in October and one in November. Since it occurs in nearby Mexico, additional sightings are possible. Larval foodplants are unknown.

Similar Species: **Brown-banded Skipper** (*page 275*) has a somewhat similar hindwing pattern but is paler and not spotted. **Hoary Skipper** (*page 269*) is spotted but lacks the hindwing bands.

Remarks: Its northeastern Mexico range extends south to Veracruz.

Spread-wing Skippers—Subfamily Pyrginae

Hoary Skipper *Carrhenes canescens*

LRGV specialty. The upperside of this pale gray-brown skipper has numerous brown spots scattered throughout and several small, transparent spots on the forewing and hindwing. The wingtip is pointed. The underside is pale brown with narrow dark-brown bands. Wingspan: 1.25–1.5 in.

When and Where: Occasional, from February to June and October to December. Most sightings are at flowering plants in gardens or in citrus groves. Larval foodplants include various mallows.

Similar Species: **Hermit** (*page 274*) and **Brown-banded** (*page 275*) **skippers** are somewhat alike. Both have a similar pale-brown color, but the Hermit Skipper is uniform brown on the upperside, without scattered glassy spots, and the Brown-banded Skipper is distinguished by numerous brown longitudinal bands.

Remarks: Scott mentions that this species feeds on the flowers of lemon trees.

Spread-wing Skippers—Subfamily Pyrginae

Glassy-winged Skipper *Xenophanes tryxus*

LRGV specialty. The upperside is gray-black with large, irregular, transparent, bluish median patches on both wings and similar large subapical spots. The hindwing has a broad bluish margin, and the fringe is slightly scalloped. The underside is similar. Wingspan: 1.25–1.5 in.

When and Where: Accidental, from July to November. It is fairly common in nearby Mexico, so additional sightings are possible. Larval foodplants consist of various mallows, including Turk's cap.

Similar Species: No other LRGV skipper has numerous large transparent patches and bluish margins.

Remarks: This tropical species feeds on various flowering plants but often perches on the ground.

Spread-wing Skippers—Subfamily Pyrginae

Texas Powdered-Skipper *Systasea pulverulenta*

The upperside has a mixed pattern of brown, black, and rust patches, separated by whitish lines, including a narrow white median line that crosses both wings. The fringes are checkered, and the hindwing is slightly scalloped. The underside is orange-brown with olive-brown patches. Wingspan: 1–1.25 in.

When and Where: Widespread but uncommon year-round. Most often observed on low-growing wildflowers or on the ground. Larval foodplants include members of the mallow family, such as Indian-mallow.

Similar Species: No other spread-wing skipper in the LRGV has a similar pattern.

Remarks: Although it is named for Texas, it is a tropical species that is more numerous in Mexico. Larvae live in nests constructed by folding over a flap of a leaf blade; full-grown larvae hibernate.

Sickle-winged Skipper *Achlyodes thraso*

Perhaps the Sickle-winged should be called "bat-winged skipper," because of its unique shape. The forewing is broad with a large pale patch on the leading edge and a slight notch below the wingtip. The dark hindwing has scattered whitish spots. Males are much darker than females, and fresh individuals have a purplish sheen. The underside is blackish and poorly marked. Wingspan: 1.5–2 in.

When and Where: Widespread and abundant year-round. It occurs in a wide variety of habitats—roadsides, gardens, and even woodlands—wherever flowering plants occur. Larval foodplants include various citrus trees, as well as pricklyash.

Similar Species: Pale Sicklewing (*page 273*) is somewhat alike but is pale brown with several darker bands across both wings.

Remarks: This tropical skipper occurs throughout most of south Texas. Larvae live in silken leaf nests.

Pale Sicklewing *Achlyodes pallida*

LRGV specialty. The upperside is mottled with olive-browns and darker browns. There is a large pale area near the leading edge of the pointed forewing. The rounded hindwing has faint dark bands. The underside is similar. Wingspan: 1.75–2.25 in.

When and Where: Accidental, from October to December. It is most likely to be found at flowering plants, but it also feeds on fruit and dung. Larval foodplants include citrus foliage.

Similar Species: Sickle-winged Skipper (*page 272*) is most alike, but it is smaller and has a smaller, more defined pale patch on the leading edge of the forewing.

Remarks: Photographs taken by Dave Hanson on October 23, 2003, represented the first U.S. record of this tropical species. See the 2003 article by Warren, et al., listed in Appendix 2, References, for more details.

Hermit Skipper *Grais stigmatica*

LRGV specialty. A fairly large, pale-brown skipper marked with scattered darker spots, including a median patch on the forewing, and three tiny, transparent subapical spots. The wingtips are pointed and the hindwings are rounded. The underside is similar, but the abdomen is yellowish and the palpi are bright yellow-orange. Wingspan: 1.75–2.25 in.

When and Where: Occasional, in April, May, and from July to November. Most sightings are at flowering plants in gardens. It sometimes rests under leaves. The only known larval foodplant in the LRGV is Runyon esenbeckia.

Similar Species: **Hoary Skipper** (*page 269*) is most alike because of its similar color, but it is smaller and has numerous small glassy spots.

Remarks: This is another tropical species that is found most years. Many authors refer to this species simply as "Hermit."

Spread-wing Skippers—Subfamily Pyrginae

Brown-banded Skipper *Timochares ruptifasciatus*

LRGV specialty. The upperside is well marked with numerous dark-brown longitudinal bands against a pale background on both the forewing and hindwing. The wingtips are pointed, and the palpi are long. The underside is mottled with orange and brown. Wingspan: 1.5–1.75 in.

When and Where: Widespread but occasional, from February to June and August to December. Most sightings are at flowering plants in gardens, but it can be found almost anywhere. The principle larval foodplant is Barbados-cherry.

Similar Species: No other pale-brown skipper is marked with numerous dark-brown longitudinal bands.

Remarks: Larvae live in rolled-leaf nests. This species occasionally strays northward in summer and fall.

White-patched Skipper *Chiomara asychis*

LRGV specialty. The upperside has a large white central patch on the broad black-and-brown hindwing. The forewing of males also has a white patch, while the female's forewing is mostly mottled black-and-white. The forewing is rounded. The underside of the hindwing is mostly white with a checkered fringe. Wingspan: 1.25–1.5 in.

When and Where: Widespread and relatively common year-round. It frequents flowering plants along woodland edges and in gardens. Larval foodplants include Barbados-cherry.

Similar Species: No other skipper has such a large white patch on the hindwing. The somewhat similar Erichson's White-Skipper (*page 285*) has a solid white band that crosses both wings and extends to the leading edge of the forewing.

Remarks: Larvae live in leaf nests. It occasionally strays northward in late summer and fall.

Spread-wing Skippers—Subfamily Pyrginae

False Duskywing *Gesta gesta*

Smaller than other duskywings, the upperside of the forewing is dark with a bluish-gray submarginal band and a pale patch on the leading edge. The hindwing has a dark basal area and a paler outer half with a very narrow white fringe. The underside is dark with pale bands. Wingspan: 1.25–1.5 in.

When and Where: Occasional, in March, April, and August. It frequents flowering plants in shaded areas, rarely visiting gardens. It commonly rests on the ground or low weedy areas. Larval food-plants include various indigos.

Similar Species: No other spread-wing skipper is similar; it is the only LRGV duskywing with bluish-gray bands.

Remarks: Although it is occasional in the LRGV, it is more numerous in brushy areas in the northern portion of south Texas. Full-grown larvae hibernate.

Horace's Duskywing *Erynnis horatius*

Sexually dimorphic, but both sexes are primarily brown with a series of white subapical spots that surround a pale patch near the leading edge of the forewing. The subapical spots are larger on females, and they have several large black basal spots. Males have black submarginal spots on both wings, while the submarginal area is pale on females. The underside is paler with a similar forewing pattern. Wingspan: 1.25–1.75 in.

When and Where: Rare, in April, October, and November. It is far more common north of the Valley, so additional sightings are possible. It is most likely to be found at flowering plants. Larval foodplants are limited to oaks.

Similar Species: No other skipper has similar features; the two other *Erynnis* duskywings in the LRGV have a white hindwing fringe.

Remarks: This skipper is sometimes known as "Brown Duskywing." Larvae live in nests of rolled or tied leaves.

Mournful Duskywing *Erynnis tristis*

This skipper is dark brown (especially fresh males), except for a bright-white hindwing fringe. The upperside of the forewing has a line of four small, white subapical spots, and three forewing spots. Barely obvious submarginal chevrons can be pale orange. The key feature is a row of white marginal spots inside the white fringe on the underside of the hindwing. Wingspan: 1.25–1.75 in.

When and Where: Uncommon, with records from every month. It is most likely to be found in gardens. Larval foodplants are limited to oaks.

Similar Species: Funereal Duskywing (*page 280*) is most alike because of the white hindwing fringe, but it is blackish and lacks the white marginal spots on the underside. The similar Northern Cloudywing (*page 249*) lacks the white hindwing fringe.

Remarks: This duskywing may be only a stray in the LRGV; its status remains uncertain. Larvae live in nests of rolled or tied leaves.

Funereal Duskywing *Erynnis funeralis*

This skipper is very dark with relatively narrow and long forewings that have a tan patch surrounded by tiny white spots near the wingtips. The blackish-brown hindwing is relatively square and unmarked except for a prominent white fringe. The underside is unmarked, except for the white hindwing fringe. Wingspan: 1.25–1.75 in.

When and Where: Widespread but uncommon year-round. Most sightings are at flowering plants along roadsides and in gardens. Larval foodplants include a wide variety of legumes, such as various vetch and lotus species.

Similar Species: Mournful Duskywing (*page 279*) is most alike but has a row of white marginal spots inside the white fringe on the underside of the hindwing. The similar Northern Cloudywing (*page 249*) lacks the white hindwing fringe.

Remarks: The Funereal Duskywing's name was derived from its dark coloration with a whitish fringe, reminiscent of a funeral shawl.

Spread-wing Skippers—Subfamily Pyrginae

Common Checkered-Skipper *Pyrgus communis*

An exact duplicate of the common White Checkered-Skipper (*page 282*), it has a variable black-and-white pattern on the upperside, and the underside is whitish and crossed by two or three irregular bands of olive patches. Wingspan: 1–1.25 in.

When and Where: Rare, with records from every month. Like the look-alike White Checkered-Skipper, it frequents low-growing wildflowers and often perches on the ground. Larval foodplants include various mallows.

Similar Species: White Checkered-Skipper (*page 282*), common in the LRGV, is identical. Where they overlap in range, as they do in the LRGV, the two can only be separated for sure by examination of the genitalia. Tropical (*page 283*) and Desert (*page 284*) checkered-skippers are also similar, but neither has a band of olive patches on the underside. The underside of the Tropical's hindwing is mottled, with three dark spots on the leading edge. Desert Checkered-Skippers have clear hindwings on the underside, except for two small black spots near the leading edge.

Remarks: The inclusion of this species is based on specimens. Further details on the differences between Common and White checkered-skippers are available in a paper by John Burns (2000), listed in Appendix 2, References.

Spread-wing Skippers—Subfamily Pyrginae

White Checkered-Skipper *Pyrgus albescens*

This little black-and-white or brown-and-white skipper has an extremely variable pattern. The upperside has a series of square white patches, edged with black or brown, on both wings, numerous submarginal spots, and a complete checkered forewing fringe. The underside of the hindwing is whitish and is crossed by irregular bands of olive patches. Wingspan: 1–1.25 in.

When and Where: Widespread and common year-round. It frequents low-growing wildflowers and often perches on the ground. It usually is a busy little skipper that flies swiftly from one site to another. Larval foodplants include various mallows.

Similar Species: Common Checkered-Skipper (*page 281*), very rare in the LRGV, is identical. It is impossible to separate the two species without examination of genitalia. The similar Tropical (*page 283*) and Desert (*page 284*) checkered-skippers are present throughout the LRGV. Neither species has bands of olive patches on the underside. The underside of the Tropical's hindwing is mottled, with three dark spots on the leading edge. Desert Checkered-Skippers have clear hindwings on the underside, except for two small black spots near the leading edge.

Remarks: Detailed descriptions of Common and White checkered-skippers are discussed in a paper by John Burns (2000), listed in Appendix 2, References.

Tropical Checkered-Skipper *Pyrgus oileus*

Like White Checkered-Skipper, the Tropical has a varied brown-and-white pattern on the upperside. Sexually dimorphic, males have a single white spot just outside a square white basal spot on the forewing. Fresh individuals have extensive bluish-white basal hairs. Females are brown with a reduced checkered pattern. Both have dark upperwing margins and checkered hindwing fringes, but there is a lack of checkering on the upper forewing fringe. The underside is marked with scattered dark spots and lines, including three dark spots on the leading edge of the hindwing. Wingspan: 1-1.25 in.

When and Where: Widespread and common year-round. It feeds on low-growing flowering plants and often rests on the ground. Larval foodplants include various mallows.

Similar Species: White (*page 282*) and Common (*page 281*) checkered-skippers are similar but have bands of olive squares on the underside. The Desert Checkered-Skipper (*page 284*) is also alike, but the underside of its hindwing is clear, except for two small, black spots near the leading edge. All three have a complete checkered forewing fringe.

Remarks: Although White and Common checkered-skippers occur throughout Texas and northward, Tropical Checkered-Skipper normally occurs in Texas only along the Gulf Coast, ranging eastward to include all of Florida.

Desert Checkered-Skipper *Pyrgus philetas*

The upperside is similar to White and Common checkered-skippers, with many white spots against a blackish or dark-brown background and a complete checkered forewing fringe. The underside of the hind-wing is pale and mainly unmarked, but it has two or three small black spots near the leading edge. Wingspan: .75–1.25 in.

When and Where: Widespread but uncommon, from March to November. This checkered-skipper prefers open, drier areas, frequently feeds on low-growing wildflowers, and often rests on the ground. Larval foodplants include various mallows.

Similar Species: Tropical Checkered-Skipper (*page 283*) is most alike but lacks the small black spots on the underside of the hindwing. White (*page 282*) and Common (*page 281*) checkered-skippers also have similar features, but both have bands of olive squares on the underside.

Remarks: Mainly an arid-land species, it is most numerous in the western portion of the LRGV.

Erichson's White-Skipper *Heliopetes domicella*

The upperside is blackish-brown with a broad white median band that uniformly crosses both wings and extends to the leading edge of the forewing. It also has a dark wing base, broad dark margins with numerous white spots, and a checkered forewing fringe. The underside of the hindwing is white with a yellowish-brown median band and a broad brown margin. Wingspan: 1–1.75 in.

When and Where: Widespread but rare, from September to December. It frequents low-growing wildflowers along roadsides and in gardens. Larval foodplants include mallows.

Similar Species: White-patched Skipper (*page 276*) is most alike, but its white patch does not extend uniformly across both wings.

Remarks: This white-skipper prefers relatively dry sites; its range extends westward to the Texas Big Bend Country.

Laviana White-Skipper *Heliopetes laviana*

The upperside is mostly white with a dark wingtip that is divided by a pale band. The hindwing margin has a series of dark chevrons, darker on females. The hindwing underside is mostly white with a distinct, blackish, sideways Y pattern on the basal area and a brown marginal patch. The forewing has a black wingtip patch. Wingspan: 1.25–1.75 in.

When and Where: Widespread and common year-round. It is often found flying swiftly from one location to another. Individuals feed on flowering plants but often perch on leaves or on the ground. Larval foodplants include various mallows.

Similar Species: The generally smaller Turk's-cap White-Skipper (*page 287*) is most alike but has reduced or absent dark margins on the upperside. Its underside lacks the sideways Y pattern. **Veined White-Skipper** (*page 288*) is also alike, but the underside has dark veins and tiny orange basal spots.

Remarks: The Laviana is sometimes known as "Tropical White-Skipper." Larvae live in leaf shelters.

Spread-wing Skippers—Subfamily Pyrginae

Turk's-cap White-Skipper *Heliopetes macaira*

The upperside is mostly white with a dark-brown wing base and a pale brown apical area, more extensive on females. Margins are pale-brown, wider on females, and have a white dash near the forewing tip. The underside of the hindwing is mostly brown, especially the darker outer portion, and there is a whitish horizontal ray on the basal area. Wingspan: 1.25–1.5 in.

When and Where: Widespread but uncommon year-round. Most sightings are along the edges of wooded areas and trails. Larval foodplants include mallows, especially Turk's cap.

Similar Species: Laviana White-Skipper (*page 286*) is similar, but the underside is mostly white with a blackish Y on the basal area of the hindwing. It has more extensive dark margins on the upperside.

Remarks: The range of this tropical skipper extends as far south as Paraguay.

Veined White-Skipper *Heliopetes arsalte*

LRGV specialty. The upperside is mostly white with dark wingtips, divided by a white spot band, and dark marginal veining. A narrow dark submarginal line is present on the hindwing. The underside is white with dark veins and tiny orange basal spots. Wingspan: 1.25–1.5 in.

When and Where: Accidental, recorded only in October. This species is fairly common in nearby Mexico, so additional sightings are possible. Larval foodplants include mallows.

Similar Species: Laviana White-Skipper (*page 286*) is most alike on the upperside. It is easily separated by the lack of dark veins and tiny orange basal spots on the underside.

Remarks: Because this species is similar to the other LRGV white-skippers, it may be overlooked.

Spread-wing Skippers—Subfamily Pyrginae

Common Streaky-Skipper *Celotes nessus*

One of the smallest skippers, it is marked with dark-brown streaks on an orange-brown background, giving it a pleated appearance. The fringes are heavily checkered. The underside is similar but paler. Wingspan: .75–1 in.

When and Where: Rare, in January and from March to October. It is most likely to be found in open areas with minimal vegetation. It feeds on low-growing wildflowers and often rests on the ground. Larval foodplants include various members of the mallow family.

Similar Species: There are no similar species in the LRGV.

Remarks: Its flight is fast, often making it difficult to follow.

Common Sootywing *Pholisora catullus*

This little skipper is glossy black with rounded wings and numerous white forewing spots, including a contrasting subapical line of five bright-white spots. White markings are also present on the head. The underside of the hindwing is all black. Wingspan: .75–1.25 in.

When and Where: Widespread but uncommon, from March to November. Most sightings are of lone individuals on or near the ground at the edge of brushy areas. Larval foodplants include various members of the Amaranthus family, such as pigweed.

Similar Species: The rare Saltbush Sootywing (*page 291*) is most alike, but it is mottled brown-and-gray and has fewer forewing spots.

Remarks: An old name for this little skipper is "Roadside Rambler."

Saltbush Sootywing   *Hesperopsis alpheus*

The upperside is mottled brown-and-gray with relatively large sub-apical spots and a brown-and-buff checkered fringe. The palpi are exceptionally long. The underside is also brown with a narrow white slash on the center of the hindwing. Wingspan: .75–1.25 in.

When and Where: Rare and local, from April to November. It is more numerous in the drier western portion of the LRGV, especially in the vicinity of saltbushes, its larval foodplant.

Similar Species: No other small spread-wing skipper has a mottled brown-and-gray upperside and checkered fringes. Common Sootywing (*page 290*) is black with more extensive white spots on the underside.

Remarks: Most sightings are of loners, but dozens have been recorded in and around a foodplant following an emergence.

Skipperlings or Intermediate Skippers— Subfamily Heteropterinae

Skipperlings are tiny skippers with broad wings, and their antennae tips lack an apiculus (extension of the club typical for skippers). The abdomen is long, and the forewings are normally held at an angle when perched. This subfamily is represented by a single species in the LRGV.

Small-spotted Skipperling *Piruna microstictus*

LRGV specialty. The upperside of this tiny skipper is black with a reddish wash and small white forewing spots. The underside is chestnut-brown with small black-rimmed, white submarginal spots. It lacks an apiculus. Wingspan: .75–1 in.

When and Where: Accidental, with a single October record. It does occur in nearby Mexico, so additional sightings are possible. Larval foodplants are grasses.

Similar Species: There are no other tiny dark LRGV skippers that lack an apiculus.

Remarks: According to Opler, this species prefers "arid subtropical chaparral" habitat, so it is most likely to occur in the western portion of the LRGV. Scott refers to this species as "Tamaulipas Skipper," after the nearby Mexican state.

Grass-skippers or Closed-wing Skippers—Subfamily Hesperiinae

These skippers are small to tiny butterflies that usually perch with their wings held upright, although they may bask with their wings fully or partially spread. Male grass-skippers also have a stigma, a patch of raised scent scales, on the upper surface of the forewing. Flight is usually fast and jerky.

Malicious Skipper *Synapte malitiosa*

LRGV specialty. The underside is pale yellowish-brown with numerous fine dark streaks, which may be difficult to see. The upperside is dark brown with a median band of yellowish-brown patches on the forewing. It also has a thin but noticeable whitish line around the eye. Wingspan: 1–1.25 in.

When and Where: Extremely rare, from April to December. Most sightings occur on low-growing wildflowers or on the ground. Larval foodplants are limited to grasses.

Similar Species: There are no other yellowish-brown skippers with fine dark streaks on the underside. The similar **Salenus** (*page 294*) and **Redundant** (*page 295*) **skippers** are reddish-brown on the underside.

Remarks: Neck refers to this little skipper as "Malicious Shady Skipper," undoubtedly due to its affinity for shaded sites. The subspecies in the LRGV is *pecta*, prompting some authors to call it "Pecta Skipper."

Grass-skippers or Closed-wing Skippers—
Subfamily Hesperiinae

Salenus Skipper *Synapte salenus*

LRGV specialty. The underside is reddish-brown on the leading portion of the hindwing with a paler trailing half that has a dark median patch. The upperside is dark brown with faint streaks. The antennae are long with a pale ring just below the black apiculus. There is a thin white line around the eye. Wingspan: 1–1.25 in.

When and Where: Accidental, from August to October. This species is fairly common in nearby Mexico, so additional sightings are possible. Larval foodplants are unknown.

Similar Species: **Malicious Skipper** (*page 293*) is most alike but is yellowish-brown on the underside of the hindwing and lacks the dark median patch. **Redundant Skipper** (*page 295*) is smaller, paler, and has a yellowish-brown patch on the upperside of the forewing.

Remarks: The first Texas record occurred after Hurricane Beulah in August 1968.

Grass-skippers or Closed-wing Skippers— Subfamily Hesperiinae

Redundant Skipper *Corticea corticea*

LRGV specialty. The underside is pale-to reddish-brown and unmarked, except for pale veins and a pale fringe. The upperside is dark brown with a median band of yellowish-brown patches on the forewing. The legs are pale, and the antennae have a pale ring just below the black apiculus. Wingspan: .75–1 in.

When and Where: There are historical records only, from September to December. Since it is present in nearby Mexico, additional sightings are possible. Larval foodplants are unknown but are probably grasses.

Similar Species: **Malicious** (*page 293*) and **Salenus** (*page 294*) **skippers** are similar, but the undersides vary. Malicious Skipper is yellowish-brown and finely streaked. Salenus Skipper has a dark median patch on the hindwing. **Double-dotted Skipper** (*page 306*) is similar on the underside but has small white median spots on the hindwing and very faint subapical spots on the forewing.

Remarks: All LRGV records occurred prior to 1980.

Grass-skippers or Closed-wing Skippers— Subfamily Hesperiinae

Pale-rayed Skipper *Vidius perigenes*

LRGV specialty. The underside is yellowish-brown with a white streak (ray) from the base to the middle of the margin on the hindwing. It has pale veins and a white fringe on the trailing edges. The upperside is dark brown and unmarked, except for a white fringe. Wingspan: 1–1.25 in.

When and Where: Occasional and local, from March to November. Most recent sightings have come from gardens at Laguna Atascosa NWR. Larval foodplants are limited to grasses.

Similar Species: Southern Skipperling (*page 311*) is similar with its underside white ray but is smaller and yellowish-orange.

Remarks: Scott mentions that this species frequents "grassy areas in thorn forest."

Grass-skippers or Closed-wing Skippers— Subfamily Hesperiinae

Violet-patched Skipper *Monca tyrtaeus*

LRGV specialty. The underside of this little skipper is rusty-brown with a bright violet-blue basal area and postmedian bands. The margins are faintly checkered. The upperside is blackish-brown with several white forewing spots and two pale subapical spots. The thorax is white, and the antennae have a white ring just below the black apiculus. Wingspan: .75–1 in.

When and Where: Occasional, with scattered records in March, from May to June, and from October to December. Most sightings are from wildflowers along roadsides, trails, and in gardens. Larval foodplants are limited to grasses.

Similar Species: A fresh Violet-patched Skipper cannot be mistaken. Worn individuals could possibly be confused with a **Fawn-spotted Skipper** (*page 300*).

Remarks: The spread of non-native Guineagrass in the LRGV may have had deleterious effects on this little skipper.

Grass-skippers or Closed-wing Skippers—
Subfamily Hesperiinae

Julia's Skipper *Nastra julia*

The underside of this plain yellowish-brown skipper has only the hint of a pale median band, and the fringes are pale. The upperside is dark brown with a few yellowish forewing spots. Wingspan: 1–1.25 in.

When and Where: Widespread and common year-round. It frequents flowering plants in varied locations, from roadsides to gardens, and it often perches on the ground. Larval foodplants are limited to grasses.

Similar Species: Swarthy Skipper (*page 299*) is most alike but has pale veins on the underside. Delaware Skipper (*page 315*) is similar but is orange, including the margins. A worn Eufala Skipper (*page 321*) is also unmarked but has a grayish wash on the underside. The male **Liris Skipper** (*page 302*) is similar but has three tiny subapical spots.

Remarks: The closely related Neamathla Skipper has not been recorded in the LRGV.

Grass-skippers or Closed-wing Skippers—
Subfamily Hesperiinae

Swarthy Skipper *Nastra lherminier*

The underside is yellowish-brown with pale veins. The upperside is dark brown with two pale median spots and three subapical spots on the forewing. Wingspan: .75–1.25 in.

When and Where: Accidental, in November. Additional records are possible, because it is fairly common in northeast Texas. Larval foodplants are limited to grasses, including little bluestem.

Similar Species: Julia's Skipper (*page 298*) is most alike but lacks the pale veins on the underside.

Remarks: This species is widespread throughout the eastern half of the United States.

Grass-skippers or Closed-wing Skippers—Subfamily Hesperiinae

Fawn-spotted Skipper *Cymaenes odilia*

LRGV specialty. The underside of the hindwing has two fawn-colored median bands; the inner band is divided into a pale central patch and a pale square patch near the upper edge. The forewing has three tiny, white subapical spots. The upperside is dark with two median spots, as well as the three subapical spots. Wingspan: .75–1.25 in.

When and Where: Widespread but uncommon year-round. Most sightings of this little skipper are on low-growing wildflowers or on the ground, especially in shaded grassy areas. Larval foodplants are limited to grasses.

Similar Species: The larger Clouded Skipper (*page 301*) is most alike, but its white subapical spots curve noticeably toward the rear. **Olive-clouded Skipper** (*page 322*) is similar but its underside hindwing patch is V-shaped and dark against a pale background.

Remarks: Sightings of this little skipper have increased in recent years.

Grass-skippers or Closed-wing Skippers— Subfamily Hesperiinae

Clouded Skipper *Lerema accius*

Color and pattern vary considerably. The underside is rich brown to gray-brown with a darker brown median band; the outer portion of the hindwing can be violet-blue on fresh individuals. The forewing has three white subapical spots that curve noticeably toward the rear. The upperside is brown with the subapical spots and two small forewing spots on males, while females have three small, glassy spots (one triangular). Wingspan: 1.5–1.75 in.

When and Where: Widespread and common year-round. It can be found almost everywhere. It often perches on leaves and grasses at varied heights above the ground. Larval foodplants include a variety of grasses.

Similar Species: The smaller **Fawn-spotted Skipper** (*page 300*) is most alike, but its white subapical spots curve only slightly toward the rear. The smaller **Olive-clouded Skipper** (*page 322*) is also similar but its white subapical spots do not curve.

Remarks: Truly one of the most numerous skippers in the LRGV, it usually is the species active earliest in the mornings.

Grass-skippers or Closed-wing Skippers— Subfamily Hesperiinae

Liris Skipper *Lerema liris*

LRGV specialty. Sexually dimorphic, the underside of males is yellowish-brown and generally unmarked except for three tiny subapical spots. Females have faint double median spots, a third spot on the leading edge, pale veins, and faintly checkered fringes. The upperside is brown with a lone forewing spot along with the three subapical spots. The legs are pale, and there is a whitish ring on the antennae below the black apiculus. Wingspan: 1–1.25 in.

When and Where: Accidental, from July to October. Since this species occurs in nearby Mexico, additional sightings are possible. It is most likely to be found at wildflowers in grassy sites. Larval foodplants are limited to grasses, including sugarcane.

Similar Species: Julia's Skipper (*page 298*) is similar to the male Liris but lacks the three subapical spots.

Remarks: Because of its use of sugarcane, a common LRGV crop, sightings are likely to continue or even increase.

Grass-skippers or Closed-wing Skippers—
Subfamily Hesperiinae

Fantastic Skipper *Vettius fantasos*

LRGV specialty. This majestic little skipper has an ivory-white underside with two dark discal spots and reddish veins on the hindwing. There are three subapical spots on the forewing. The upperside is blackish with a reddish sheen, and it has three large, whitish median spots on the hindwing, several smaller white spots on the forewing, and broad white margins. The abdomen and throat are white, and the legs are yellow. Wingspan: 1–1.25 in.

When and Where: Accidental, from October to December. It is relatively common in nearby Mexico, so additional sightings are possible. Larval foodplants are limited to grasses.

Similar Species: No other skipper can match this "fantastic" species.

Remarks: This is one of the many stray skippers that were recorded during the amazing fall season of 2003.

Grass-skippers or Closed-wing Skippers—
Subfamily Hesperiinae

Green-backed Ruby-eye *Perichares philetes*

LRGV specialty. This large skipper has an iridescent green thorax and abdomen and ruby-red eyes. The underside is dark brown with purplish basal, median, and rear patches. The fringes are checkered. The upperside is dark brown with pale-yellow spots on the forewing. The legs are yellow. Wingspan: 1.5–2.25 in.

When and Where: Accidental, in November and December. The species occurs in nearby Mexico, so additional sightings are possible. Larval foodplants consist of grasses, including sugarcane.

Similar Species: No other skipper has the combination of green body and ruby-red eyes.

Remarks: One of the most bizarre skippers! Scott refers to this species as "Gaudy Skipper."

Grass-skippers or Closed-wing Skippers—
Subfamily Hesperiinae

Osca Skipper *Rhinthon osca*

LRGV specialty. This is a bulky skipper with a chocolate-brown underside and three small, white median spots on the hindwing; the forewing has four median spots (one is very large and square), and three tiny subapical spots. The upperside is darker brown with a similar pattern. Wingspan: 1.5–1.75 in.

When and Where: Accidental, recorded only in October. It is a stray, based on the records, but since its larval foodplants include sugarcane, common in the Valley, it may become a more regular visitor or a resident.

Similar Species: Brazilian Skipper (*page 323*) is somewhat similar but is larger and paler.

Remarks: Osca Skipper was earlier considered a subspecies of Cuban Skipper, a species now limited to the Antilles.

Grass-skippers or Closed-wing Skippers— Subfamily Hesperiinae

Double-dotted Skipper *Decinea percosius*

LRGV specialty. The underside is dark reddish-brown with one to four small white median spots on the hindwing, and three very faint subapical spots on the forewing. The upperside is dark brown with several whitish spots, including two large median squares, two smaller spots, and three small subapical spots. The fringes are pale. Wingspan: .75-1 in.

When and Where: Occasional and local, from March to December. The majority of sightings come from Sabal Palm Sanctuary. Larval foodplants are limited to grasses.

Similar Species: **Redundant Skipper** (*page 295*) and **Hidden-ray Skipper** (*page 307*) are similar on the underside but lack the white spots.

Remarks: Neck refers to this species as "Percosius Skipper" and states that it is "very common some years."

Grass-skippers or Closed-wing Skippers— Subfamily Hesperiinae

Hidden-ray Skipper *Conga chydaea*

LRGV specialty. The underside is brown with a yellowish tinge on the unmarked hindwing. The forewing has a short white streak (ray) near the trailing edge. The upperside is blackish-brown and usually unmarked; faint forewing and subapical spots are possible. Wingspan: .75–1.25 in.

When and Where: Accidental, from July to October. Its presence in nearby Mexico suggests that additional sightings are possible. Larval foodplants are unknown.

Similar Species: **Double-dotted Skipper** (*page 306*) is similar, especially if worn, but it has one or more small median spots on the underside of the hindwing.

Remarks: This little tropical skipper ranges south to Argentina.

Grass-skippers or Closed-wing Skippers— Subfamily Hesperiinae

Least Skipper *Ancyloxypha numitor*

This little pale-orange skipper has numerous pale veins on the underside of its broad hindwing. The upperside is orange-brown with broad blackish margins. Flight is weak and fluttering. Wingspan: .75–1 in.

When and Where: Rare and local, from March to November. It prefers moist sites, such as ditches and wetland edges. Larval foodplants are limited to grasses.

Similar Species: Tropical Least Skipper (*page 309*) is most alike, but the underside lacks the numerous faint veins. It has a broad brown outer margin on the upperside. Orange Skipperling (*page 310*) lacks obvious veins on the underside and has a noticeably longer abdomen. The smaller Southern Skipperling (*page 311*) has a pale ray on the underside of the hindwing.

Remarks: This little skipper occurs throughout the eastern half of the United States.

Grass-skippers or Closed-wing Skippers—
Subfamily Hesperiinae

Tropical Least Skipper *Ancyloxypha arene*

The underside is pale orange with a pale ray along the inner margin of the hindwing. The upperside is bright orange with a brown wingtip and hindwing margin. Flight is weak and fluttering. Wingspan: .75–1.25 in.

When and Where: Rare and local, recorded only in July. It is most likely to be found at moist, grassy sites. Larval foodplants include grasses.

Similar Species: Least Skipper (*page 308*) is most alike but has numerous pale veins on the underside. Orange Skipperling (*page 310*) is similar but the upperside of the hindwing lacks the broad brown margin. Southern Skipperling (*page 311*) is smaller and has an obvious pale ray in the middle of the hindwing on the underside.

Remarks: This little skipper occurs in the United States only along the Texas-Mexican border westward to southeast Arizona.

Grass-skippers or Closed-wing Skippers—
Subfamily Hesperiinae

Orange Skipperling *Copaeodes aurantiaca*

The underside is yellowish-orange and unmarked except for a dark fringe. The upperside is similar, but males have a heavy black stigma at the base of the forewing. The long orange abdomen extends beyond the hindwing. Wingspan: .75–1 in.

When and Where: Widespread but uncommon year-round. It can be absent for extended periods. Most sightings are of individuals perched on low shrubs in a variety of habitats. Larval foodplants consist of various grasses, including Bermudagrass and several grama grasses.

Similar Species: Least Skipper (*page 308*) is most alike. It has a broad hindwing with pale veins, and the upperside of the hindwing is orange with a broad blackish margin. Southern Skipperling (*page 311*) is also similar but has a pale ray that runs the length of the underside of the hindwing. The similar Tropical Least Skipper (*page 309*) has a pale ray along the inner margin of the hindwing.

Remarks: This little orange skipper is resident throughout most of Texas.

Grass-skippers or Closed-wing Skippers—
Subfamily Hesperiinae

Southern Skipperling *Copaeodes minima*

This tiny yellowish-orange skipper has a whitish ray running the length of the hindwing on the underside. The upperside is orange-brown with a blackish basal area and hindwing fringe. Females have dark veins. Wingspan: .5–.75 in.

When and Where: Widespread and common year-round. It is most likely to be found in open areas with low grasses. Larval foodplants are limited to grasses, including Bermudagrass.

Similar Species: Although Least (*page 308*) and Tropical Least (*page 309*) skippers and Orange Skipperling (*page 310*) are somewhat alike, none of them has the pronounced whitish ray on the middle of the hindwing underside. **Pale-rayed Skipper** (*page 296*) has a white ray, but the Pale-rayed is much larger and yellowish-brown.

Remarks: This is the smallest of all the North American skippers. Its range extends eastward through most of the southeastern United States.

Grass-skippers or Closed-wing Skippers— Subfamily Hesperiinae

Fiery Skipper *Hylephila phyleus*

The underside of the hindwing is yellowish-orange with dark fringes and numerous scattered brown spots. The upperside is sexually dimorphic: male hindwings are mostly yellowish-orange with a black base and blackish-brown "toothed" margins; female hindwings are orange with black streaks and wide black margins. The antennae are noticeably short. Wingspan: 1–1.25 in.

When and Where: Widespread and common year-round. Several can often be found feeding on a single flowering shrub. Larval foodplants are limited to grasses, including Bermudagrass.

Similar Species: Whirlabout (*page 313*) males are most alike, but the dark spots on the underside are larger and paired. Sachem (*page 316*) can also look alike, but it is brown to yellowish-gray. Sachem males have a large black forewing stigma, and females have a large glassy median spot on the upperside.

Remarks: The Fiery's range extends west to California and east through most of the eastern half of the United States.

Grass-skippers or Closed-wing Skippers— Subfamily Hesperiinae

Whirlabout *Polites vibex*

Sexually dimorphic, the underside of males is pale yellow with several large brown spots—two aligned submarginal pairs and a smaller central pair—on the hindwing. The underside of females is pale to dark brown with larger paired dark spots. The upperside of males has an orange center with noticeable black veins, broad black hindwing margins, a narrow orange fringe, and a line of black squares (including stigma) on the forewing. The upperside of females is uniformly dark brown, except for two forewing spots and three subapical spots. Wingspan: 1–1.25 in.

Male

When and Where: Widespread and common year-round. It frequents flowering plants in weedy habitats. Larval foodplants are limited to grasses, including Bermudagrass.

Similar Species: Fiery Skipper males (*page 312*) are similar to male Whirlabouts, but the underside hindwing spots are smaller and are not paired.

Female

Remarks: This skipper occurs only in the southeastern United States and eastern Mexico.

Southern Broken-Dash *Wallengrenia otho*

The underside can vary from brownish-yellow to reddish-brown with a median band of pale spots, often shaped like a "3." The upperside differs by sex: forewings of males are orange-brown with a black stigma and a yellowish median dash; forewings of females are dark brown with two yellowish median dashes, three subapical spots, and a gray fringe. Wingspan: 1–1.25 in.

When and Where: Widespread and common year-round. It feeds on flowering plants in a variety of habitats. Larval foodplants include various grasses.

Similar Species: Common Mellana (*page 317*) and Delaware Skipper (*page 315*) are most alike, but both are yellowish-orange instead of reddish-brown. Common Mellana may have a very faint postmedian band, but it is not shaped like a "3." Delaware Skipper lacks a spot-band on the underside of the hindwing. Dun Skipper (*page 318*) can be similar on the underside but also lacks a spot-band; most Dun Skippers have gold on the head.

Remarks: The southern subspecies *curassavica* occurs in the LRGV, and some lepidopterists believe it is a separate species. Northern Broken-Dash does not occur in south Texas.

Grass-skippers or Closed-wing Skippers— Subfamily Hesperiinae

Delaware Skipper *Anatrytone logan*

The underside, including the fringe, is yellowish-orange and unmarked. The upperside is orange with a broad dark hindwing base and margins (black on males) and black veins; females have a black cell bar. It has orange legs and an orange patch on the inner half of the apiculus. Wingspan: 1–1.75 in.

When and Where: Accidental, reported only in June. It is found regularly to the north and west of the LRGV, so additional sightings are possible. Larval foodplants are limited to grasses.

Similar Species: Common Mellana (*page 317*) is most alike but has a faint postmedian band on the underside and a dark fringe. The similar Southern Broken-Dash (*page 314*) has a faint postmedian band and a gray fringe. The yellowish-brown Julia's Skipper (*page 298*) is similar on the underside but has a pale median band and pale fringes.

Remarks: Pyle reports that populations of this species "may differ in color as well as in behavior at different times of day."

Grass-skippers or Closed-wing Skippers—
Subfamily Hesperiinae

Sachem *Atalopedes campestris*

This is a fairly large and sexually dimorphic skipper. Both sexes can vary from a warm brown to yellowish-gray, but the underside of the male's hindwing can range from having almost no markings to having a yellowish median patch with dark margins and a broad subapical line. The underside of females is marked with pale squares that form a V-pattern (pointed toward the rear). The upperside of males is brown and orange with a heavy black stigma on the forewing. The female is similar but has several large glassy square forewing spots and a subapical line. Wingspan: 1.25–1.75 in.

When and Where: Widespread and common year-round. It frequents flowering plants in varied habitats. Larval foodplants include a variety of grasses, such as Bemudagrass and crabgrass.

Similar Species: Although this species is generally larger than most of the other grass-skippers, worn Sachems can be mistaken for several other species. The smaller Fiery Skipper (*page 312*) is somewhat alike, for instance, but is usually bright yellowish-orange.

Remarks: Sachem may be misidentified more than any of the other LRGV skippers.

Grass-skippers or Closed-wing Skippers—Subfamily Hesperiinae

Common Mellana *Quasimellana eulogius*

LRGV specialty. The underside of this little skipper is yellow to pale orange with a faint postmedian band, often difficult to see. The upperside is sexually dimorphic. Males have a pair of orange wedge-shaped median patches and a subapical line on the hindwing. Females are brown with several pale forewing spots and a median line of yellowish streaks. Wingspan: 1–1.25 in.

When and Where: Occasional, from April to February. It is most often found on flowering shrubs, especially crucitas, in fall. Larval foodplants are unknown.

Similar Species: Delaware Skipper (*page 315*) is most alike but is brighter orange and lacks a faint postmedian band. Southern Broken-Dash (*page 314*), at least the yellowish form, is also alike but has a larger, more obvious median band on the underside of the hindwing. (Worn Southern Broken-Dash individuals are difficult to differentiate; look for the Common Mellana's more swept-back forewing when perched.) Julia's Skipper (*page 298*) is yellowish-brown on the underside with pale fringes.

Remarks: Some earlier authors refer to this species as "Eulogius Skipper," and they considered it a stray only. But increased sightings in recent years suggest that it may now breed in the LRGV.

Grass-skippers or Closed-wing Skippers— Subfamily Hesperiinae

Dun Skipper *Euphyes vestris*

The underside is pale brown and unmarked; the head and palpi are usually gold. The male's upperside is brown—darkest on the trailing portion of the forewing—with a black stigma. Females have two white median spots on the forewing and a pair of subapical spots on the hindwing. Wingspan: 1–1.25 in.

When and Where: Widespread but occasional, from March to December. It is most likely to be found on wildflowers along roadsides, especially near moist areas. Larval foodplants include sedges.

Similar Species: Other pale, mainly unmarked skippers, such as Julia's (*page 298*) and **Double-dotted** (*page 306*), Southern Broken-Dash (*page 314*), and even a worn Sachem (*page 316*) are similar, but none of them has a gold head.

Remarks: The only other Texas skipper with a gold/orange head is the Orange-headed Roadside-Skipper, which does not occur in the LRGV. Some authors once referred to the Dun Skipper as "Sedge Witch."

Grass-skippers or Closed-wing Skippers— Subfamily Hesperiinae

Nysa Roadside-Skipper *Amblyscirtes nysa*

This is a tiny, well-marked skipper with a mottled brown, gray, and black underside, including a large black square on the lower edge of the hindwing and strongly checkered fringes. The upperside is blackish with one median forewing spot and three subapical spots. Wingspan: .75–1 in.

When and Where: Widespread but uncommon, from February to October. It is most likely to be found in open areas, including trails and roadways. Larval foodplants are limited to grasses, including crabgrass and St. Augustinegrass.

Similar Species: No other little LRGV skipper has a similar underwing pattern.

Remarks: It is most active during the morning hours but seems to disappear soon thereafter.

Celia's Roadside-Skipper *Amblyscirtes celia*

The underside is gray-brown with several scattered dull-white hindwing spots, three white subapical spots, and a brown-and-white checkered fringe. The upperside is dark brown with two whitish forewing spots and faint subapical spots. Wingspan: 1–1.25 in.

When and Where: Widespread and common year-round. It frequents flowering plants in a wide variety of habitats. Larval foodplants are limited to grasses, including Guineagrass and St. Augustinegrass.

Similar Species: No other little gray-brown skipper in the LRGV has a similar dotted underwing pattern.

Remarks: The very similar Bell's Roadside-Skipper does not occur in south Texas.

Grass-skippers or Closed-wing Skippers—Subfamily Hesperiinae

Dotted Roadside-Skipper *Amblyscirtes eos*

This little blackish-brown skipper has scattered white dots, each bordered with black, on the underside of the hindwing. The forewing has three white forewing spots, three white subapical spots, and a black-and-white checkered fringe. The upperside is darker with a V-pattern of small white spots. Wingspan: .75–1.25 in.

When and Where: Accidental, dates unknown. It is most likely in the drier western portion of the LRGV. Larval foodplants are limited to grasses, particularly panicgrass.

Similar Species: Celia's Roadside-Skipper (*page 319*) is most alike, but its hindwing spots are not edged with black.

Remarks: Scott refers to this species as "Starry Little Skipper."

Grass-skippers or Closed-wing Skippers—Subfamily Hesperiinae

Eufala Skipper *Lerodea eufala*

The underside varies from pale "suede" gray to a greenish-gray and is generally unmarked, although some have a faint median spot-band. The forewing has two pale subapical spots, and the eye is edged with white. The upperside is brown with several white forewing spots, a subapical line, and gray margins. This species has a habit of giving two rapid wing-quivers after landing. Wingspan: .75–1.25 in.

When and Where: Widespread and common year-round. It feeds on flowering plants in almost every habitat. Larval foodplants are limited to grasses, including Bermudagrass, Johnsongrass, and sorghum.

Similar Species: Julia's Skipper (*page 298*) is most alike but is yellowish-brown instead of grayish on the underside.

Remarks: This trim little skipper is widely distributed throughout the southern United States and southward.

Grass-skippers or Closed-wing Skippers— Subfamily Hesperiinae

Olive-clouded Skipper *Lerodea dysaules*

LRGV specialty. The underside is olive-brown with a wide, pale-edged, dark, V-shaped median patch (pointed toward the trailing edge) on the hindwing. The forewing has an uneven subapical bar. The upperside is pale brown, slightly darker on the outer edge, and has a pale fringe and several white forewing spots, including one large median spot and an uneven subapical bar. Wingspan: .75–1.25 in.

When and Where: Widespread but uncommon year-round, most numerous from June to December. It feeds on flowering plants but often perches on the ground. Larval foodplants are probably grasses.

Similar Species: Fawn-spotted Skipper (*page 300*) is most alike, but its underwing patches are pale against a dark background. The larger Clouded Skipper (*page 301*) is also similar, but the subapical spots curve noticeably toward the rear.

Remarks: Once lumped with Violet-clouded Skipper (found only in Arizona), Olive-clouded Skipper is now a separate species that enters the United States only in the LRGV.

Grass-skippers or Closed-wing Skippers— Subfamily Hesperiinae

Brazilian Skipper *Calpodes ethlius*

This large skipper has a pale reddish-brown underside with three (typically) glassy postmedian spots on the rounded hindwing; the forewing is noticeably long. The upperside is blackish-brown with several glassy forewing spots and three median chevrons on the hindwing. Wingspan: 1.75–2.25 in.

When and Where: Uncommon and local year-round. Most sightings are near cannas, its larval foodplant. It perches on nearby leaves and even on the ground and feeds on a variety of flowering plants, including those with deep tubular flowers.

Similar Species: No other brown skipper is so large. The very rare **Osca Skipper** (*page 305*) is smaller and chocolate-brown on the underside.

Remarks: Larvae and pupae live in rolled-leaf nests and feed mainly after dark. Adults were once known as "Canna Skipper," because of their larval foodplant.

Grass-skippers or Closed-wing Skippers—
Subfamily Hesperiinae

Obscure Skipper *Panoquina panoquinoides*

The underside is pale brown with three aligned white median spots (the two lower spots smaller and close together) and pale veins. The upperside is brown with several white forewing spots, including a large triangular median spot and a pair of subapical spots. Wingspan: 1–1.25 in.

When and Where: Uncommon and local year-round. It is most likely to be found on shrubs near the coast and is rare farther inland. Its larval foodplant is limited to saltgrass.

Similar Species: No other LRGV skipper is similar.

Remarks: The name—Obscure Skipper—is appropriate; it is often obscure, in spite of being present in good numbers at key locations.

Grass-skippers or Closed-wing Skippers—
Subfamily Hesperiinae

Ocola Skipper *Panoquina ocola*

The underside has a faint whitish median band on the squared brown hindwing; fresh individuals have a purplish sheen, which appears darker, on the rear portion. The forewing is noticeably long. The upperside is brown with two forewing spots—including a large white median arrowhead—and two subapical spots. Wingspan: 1.25–1.5 in.

When and Where: Widespread and common year-round. It is most numerous in late summer and fall. It feeds on flowering plants in a wide variety of habitats. Larval foodplants are limited to grasses, including sugarcane.

Similar Species: Purple-washed Skipper (*page 327*) is most alike, but the median spot-band on the underside of the hindwing is comprised of distinct white spots and the hindwing, especially on fresh individuals, is noticeably purple. **Hecebolus Skipper** (*page 326*) is also similar but has two small, flat white spots, one above the other, behind the arrowhead on the forewing upperside.

Remarks: An earlier name for this skipper was "Long-winged Skipper," due to its unusually long forewing.

Grass-skippers or Closed-wing Skippers— Subfamily Hesperiinae

Hecebolus Skipper *Panoquina hecebola*

LRGV specialty. The underside of the noticeably rounded hindwing is yellow-brown with faint veins and shows no darkening toward the rear; some individuals have a purplish sheen. The much longer forewing has three median spots, including a central arrowhead mark, and faint subapical spots. The upperside is reddish-brown with similar spots on the forewing. The key distinguishing feature is two small, flat, white spots, one above and the other behind the arrowhead. Wingspan: 1.25–1.5 in.

When and Where: Rare, from July to December. Most sightings occur in fall. The majority are of individuals feeding on crucitas or asters in fields. Larval foodplants are unknown, but it is likely sugarcane.

Similar Species: Ocola Skipper (*page 325*) is similar, but the median spots on the upperside of the forewing are limited to a central arrowhead and a single flattened spot.

Remarks: This is another tropical skipper that has been increasingly reported in recent years.

Grass-skippers or Closed-wing Skippers—
Subfamily Hesperiinae

Purple-washed Skipper *Panoquina sylvicola*

LRGV specialty. The underside of the brown hindwing, crossed with a median band of distinct white spots, has an obvious purplish sheen. The forewing is extremely long with broad subapical spots. The upperside is dark brown with several forewing spots, including a large median arrowhead and an elongated white spot in the forewing cell. Wingspan: 1.25–1.5 in.

When and Where: Widespread but occasional, from August to January. It is most likely to be found at flowering shrubs, especially crucitas. Larval foodplants are limited to grasses, including sugarcane.

Similar Species: Ocola Skipper (*page 325*) is most alike but lacks the elongated spot in the forewing cell. **Hecebolus Skipper** (*page 326*) is similar on the upperside but lacks the median spot-band on the underside. The stray **Evans' Skipper** (*page 328*) also has a very long forewing, but the underside of its purplish hindwing is marked with a broad whitish band and faint whitish veins.

Remarks: Sightings of this skipper have increased in recent years.

Grass-skippers or Closed-wing Skippers— Subfamily Hesperiinae

Evans' Skipper *Panoquina fusina*

LRGV specialty. The underside of the hindwing has a deep-purplish sheen throughout, except for a broad whitish median band, pale veins, and a pale-orange fringe. The forewing is extremely long and also has a purplish sheen. The upperside is dark brown with numerous amber spots, including a pair of arrowheads and two subapical spots. Wingspan: 1.5–1.75 in.

When and Where: Accidental, in October and November. It is fairly common in nearby Mexico, so additional sightings are possible. Most local sightings have come from gardens; it commonly rests on the ground. Larval foodplants are probably grasses, including sugarcane.

Similar Species: **Purple-washed Skipper** (*page 327*) is most alike but is smaller and lacks the extensive deep-purplish sheen and the broad whitish median band on the underside of the hindwing.

Remarks: This skipper was earlier regarded as only a subspecies of *Panoquina fusina*; it was then known as "White-barred Skipper."

Grass-skippers or Closed-wing Skippers—
Subfamily Hesperiinae

Violet-banded Skipper *Nyctelius nyctelius*

LRGV specialty. The pale-brown underside is well-marked on fresh individuals with a broad dark median band, a narrow postmedian band, and a black spot on the leading edge of the hindwing; some individuals have a violet cast. The forewing is narrow and extends well beyond the rather square hindwing. The upperside is dark brown with several forewing spots, including a large square white median spot. Wingspan: 1.25–1.75 in.

When and Where: Occasional, in May and from September to February. This is another of the fall specialties that is most often encountered feeding on crucitas in various habitats. Larval foodplants are limited to grasses, including sugarcane and corn.

Similar Species: **Fawn-spotted** (*page 300*) and **Olive-clouded** (*page 322*) **skippers** are similar but are smaller and lack the black spot on the leading edge of the hindwing underside.

Remarks: This skipper occurs in Mexico, southward to Argentina, and also in the West Indies.

Giant-Skippers—Subfamily Megathyminae

These large skippers with muscular bodies are able to fly extremely fast. Yet they do not migrate. They seldom, if ever, feed at flowers but do sip moisture at puddles.

Yucca Giant-Skipper *Megathymus yuccae*

The underside is blackish with frosted-gray outer margins and white spots, including a broad triangle and a smaller line on the leading edge of the hindwing. The upperside is black on males and dark brown on females, both with broad yellow postmedian bands and a checkered fringe. Wingspan: 2.5–2.75 in.

When and Where: Occasional and local, from February to April. It is most often seen in flight, but careful observers can sometimes locate a perched individual on vegetation near Spanish daggers, the larval foodplant. They do not feed at flowers. The Boca Chica area, east of Sabal Palm Sanctuary, is the best bet for finding this unusual skipper.

Similar Species: No other skipper is so large and so fast a flier.

Remarks: Manfreda Giant-Skipper, which once resided in areas of manfreda, apparently has been extirpated from the LRGV but is described on page 331.

Manfreda Giant-Skipper *Stallingsia maculosa*

The underside of the hindwing is dark brown with a gray dusting on the margin. The upperside is dark brown to black with a postmedian line of pale-orange spots on the forewing and faint spots on the hindwing. The fringes are checkered. Wingspan: 1.75-2 in.

When and Where: There are historic records only, in May and from September to November. It is likely extirpated from the LRGV and may also be extirpated from all of its south Texas range. Larval foodplants are limited to manfreda, a succulent plant that has been severely decimated throughout its range.

Similar Species: The related Yucca Giant-Skipper (*page 330*) is larger and black-and-gray on the underside and brown with large yellow hindwing patches on the upperside.

Remarks: Two flight periods have been recorded, in April and May and again in September and October.

Hypothetical Species

Below are photographs of some of the hypothetical butterfly species, which are not fully documented but are still possible, in the Lower Rio Grande Valley. See Appendix 3, Butterfly Checklist for the Lower Rio Grande Valley, for a more complete list with scientific names.

Eastern Tiger Swallowtail
Wingspan: 3.5–6.5 in.

Palamedes Swallowtail
Wingspan: 4.75–5.25 in.

Mexican Dartwhite
Wingspan: 1.75–2.25 in.

Mexican Cycadian
Wingspan: 1.5–2 in.

Creamy Stripe-Streak
Wingspan: 1.25–1.5 in.

Ardys Crescent
Wingspan: 1.25–1.5 in.

Huastecan Crescent
Wingspan: 1–1.25 in.

Orange Mapwing
Wingspan: 1.75–2.5 in.

Common Morpho
Wingspan: 2.45–6.5 in.

Rainbow Skipper
Wingspan: 1–2.5 in.

Silver-spotted Skipper
Wingspan: 1.75–2.5 in.

Hayhurst's Scallopwing
Wingspan: 1–1.25 in.

Mexican Sootywing
Wingspan: .75–1.25 in.

Ubiquitous Skipper
Wingspan: 1–1.5 in.

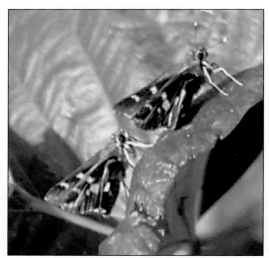
Chestnut-marked Skipper
Wingspan: 1.25–1.5 in.

Appendix 1

Glossary

Angled: shape of the hindwing that has a tail-like extension.

Antennae: a pair of sensory appendages located on the head.

Apex: tip of the wing.

Apical: the area near the wingtip.

Basal: the portion of the wing nearest the body.

Bask: to perch in a sunny site to absorb the warm sunlight, usually early in the morning.

Cell: the interior area of a wing, enclosed by veins.

Club: the expanded tip of the antennae.

Costal fold: a narrow flap of scent scales, used for sexual attraction, located near the front edge of the forewing.

Dimorphic: having two distinct forms, such as male and female or winter and summer.

Discal bar: a line on the center of the wing.

Dorsal: pertaining to the upperside.

Eyespot: a round spot on the wing, often with a darker or lighter interior, against a contrasting background.

Falcate: slightly hooked, referring to the wingtip.

Foodplant: plant utilized for egg laying, on which the larvae feed.

Forewing: the front wing.

Form: appearance, such as a summer and a winter form.

Fringe: the outer edge of the wing margin.

Hindwing: the rear wing.

Larva: the caterpillar; an immature butterfly.

Lobe: an extension of the anal angle of the hindwing.

Margin: the outer edge of the wing.

Median: the middle area of the wing.

Palpus: a facial appendage used for sensing and for cleaning the proboscis.

Pheromone: a sexual scent to attract the opposite sex.

Proboscis: a coiled tube that extends from the mouth, used for feeding.

Ray: a narrow band of color that contrasts with the background color.

Scales: the tiny shingle-like structures that provide color.

Stigma: a patch of specialized scales on the forewing that produce a scent, used to attract a mate.

Submargin: the section of the wing near the edge.

Underside: referring to the view of the ventral side.

Upperside: referring to the view of the dorsal side.

Vein: a narrow tube in a wing that provides structural support.

Ventral: pertaining to the underside.

Appendix 2

References

Bordelon, Charles, & Ed Knudson. 2002. *Illustrated Checklist of Leoptera of the Lower Rio Grande Valley. Part 1: Butterflies.* Houston: Texas Lepidoptera Survey.

Bordelon, Charles, & Ed Knudson. 2003. Anastrus sempiternus Butler & Druce, a New Record for Texas and the USA. *News Lep. Soc.* 45(1):7.

Brock, Jim P., and Kenn Kaufman. 2003. *Butterflies of North America.* NY: Houghton Mifflin Co.

Burns, John M. 2000. Pyrgus communis and Pyrgus albescens (Hesperiidae: Pyrginae) Are Separate Transcontinental Species with Variable but Diagnostic Valves. *J. Lep. Soc.* 54(2):52-71.

Glassberg, Jeffrey. 1999. *Butterflies through Binoculars: The East.* NY: Oxford Univ. Press.

Glassberg, Jeffrey. 2001. Cracking the Code. *American Butterflies* 9(4):16-27.

Grassberg, Jeffrey. 2002. Go Get Set On Your Marks: Yellows. Part 2. *American Butterflies* 10(2): 24-33.

Glassberg, Jeffrey. 2003. Go Get Set On Your Marks: Super Sulphurs. *American Butterflies* 11(3):14-25.

Hanson, David J., Ed Knudson, and Charles Bordelon. 2003. Phocides belus Godman & Salvin (Hesperidae), New to US and Texas. *News Lep. Soc.* 45(2):42-43.

Howe, Willam H. 1975. *The Butterflies of North America.* NY: Doubleday & Co., Inc.

Kendall, Roy O. 1976. Larval Foodplants and Life History Notes for Some Metalmarks (Lepidoptera: Riodinidae) from Mexico and Texas. *Bulletin Allyn Museum.* 32:1-12.

Kendall, Roy O., and William W. McGuire. 1984. Some New and Rare Records of Lepidoptera Found in Texas. *Bulletin Allyn Museum.* 86:1-50.

McGuire, W. W., and Mike A. Rickard. 1974. An Annotated Checklist of the Butterflies (Lepidoptera: Rhopalocera) of Bentsen-Rio Grande Valley State Park and Vicinity. Mission, Tx: Texas Parks & Wildlife Dept. (photocopy)

Neck, Raymond W. 1996. *A Field Guide to Butterflies of Texas.* Houston: Gulf Publishing Co.

North American Butterfly Association. 2001. *Checklist & English Names of North American Butterflies Second Edition.* Morrison, NJ: North American Butterfly Association.

Opler, Paul A., and Vichai Malikul. 1998. *A Field Guide to Eastern Butterflies.* Boston: Houghton Mifflin Co.

Opler, Paul A., and Andrew D. Warren. 2002. *Butterflies of North America. 2. Scientific Names List for Butterfly Species of North America, North of Mexico.* Fort Collins, Co: C.P. Gillette Museum of Arthropod Diversity, Colorado State Univ.

Pyle, Robert Michael. 1995. *National Audubon Society Field Guide to North American Butterflies.* NY: Alfred A. Knopf.

Scott, James A. 1986. *The Butterflies of North America: A Natural History and Field Guide.* Stanford, CA: Stanford Univ. Press.

Stewart, Bob, Priscilla Brodkin, and Hank Brodkin. 2001. *Butterflies of Arizona: A Photographic Guide.* Arcata, Ca: West Coast Lady Press.

Warren, Andrew D. 1977. Urbanus belli (Hesperiidae: Pyrginae): A New Record for the United States. *News Lepid. Soc.* 39(3):41.

Warren, Andrew D., David J. Hanson, Ed Knudson, and Charles Bordelon. 2003. Achlyodes pallida (Hesperiidae): A New Record for the United States. *News Lep. Soc.* 45(4):128-30.

Wauer, Roland H. 2003. Rare & Unusual Texas Butterfly Records. *News Lepid. Soc.* 45(1):5,6&9.

Appendix 3

Butterfly Checklist for the Lower Rio Grande Valley

(Includes Starr, Hidalgo, and Cameron counties.)

The following checklist follows the taxonomic order established by the North American Butterfly Association (NABA). It utilizes NABA common and scientific names. Alternate common names are given in parentheses. When scientific names utilized by Opler and Warren (2002) differ, they are included in brackets.

LRGV specialties are listed in **boldface**.

The status codes represent the relative abundance of species likely to be found in the seasons and locations where they occur. If known, months in which the species has been recorded are included in parentheses. See the text for more information on locations and/or habitats where the species is likely to be found.

Status codes:

A = abundant: many can be expected on most visits to appropriate locations. Examples include Cloudless Sulphur, American Snout, and Queen.

C = common: several can be expected on most visits to appropriate locations. Examples include Pipevine Swallowtail, Southern Dogface, and Bordered Patch.

U = uncommon: a few can often be found on most visits to appropriate locations. Examples include Giant Swallowtail, Great Purple Hairstreak, and Mexican Bluewing.

O = occasional: one or a very few can sometimes be found on visits to appropriate locations. Examples include Polydamas Swallowtail, Giant White, and Zilpa Longtail.

R = rare: one to several occur every few years only. Examples include Ruby-spotted Swallowtail, Blue-eyed Sailor, and Falcate Skipper.

X = accidental: a nonbreeding stray, may never be found again. Examples include Dark Kite-Swallowtail, Aquamarine Hairstreak, and Red Cracker.

H = historical: records prior to 1980 only.

L = local: one to many are possible but normally only at specific locations. Examples include Xami Hairstreak, Definite Patch, and Yucca Giant-Skipper.

Swallowtails—Family Papilionidae

Swallowtails—Subfamily Papilioninae

___ Pipevine Swallowtail *Battus philenor*: C (Jan–Dec)

___ **Polydamas Swallowtail** *Battus polydamas*: O (Mar–Jan)

___ **Dark Kite-Swallowtail** *Eurytides philolaus*: X (Jul, Oct)

___ Black Swallowtail *Papilio polyxenes*: U (Jan–Dec)

___ **Thoas Swallowtail** *Papilio thoas*: X (Apr–Jul, Sep, Oct)

___ Giant Swallowtail *Papilio cresphontes*: C (Jan–Dec)

___ Ornythion Swallowtail *Papilio ornythion*: R (Mar–June, Aug–Nov)

___ **Broad-banded Swallowtail** *Papilio astyalus*: X (Apr, Aug–Oct)

___ **Three-tailed Swallowtail** *Papilio pilumnus*: H (May)

___ **Magnificent (Abderus) Swallowtail** *Papilio garamas*: H (Sep, Oct)

___ **Pink-spotted Swallowtail** *Papilio pharnaces* [*P. rogeri*]: X (Apr)

___ **Ruby-spotted Swallowtail** *Papilio anchisiades*: R, L (Apr–Jul, Sep–Dec)

Whites and Sulphurs—Family Pieridae

Whites—Subfamily Pierinae

____ **Florida (Tropical) White** *Appias drusilla*: O (Mar–May, Jul–Nov)
____ **Mountain White** *Leptophobia aripa*: X (Oct)
____ Checkered White *Pontia protodice*: C (Jan–Dec)
____ Cabbage White *Pieris rapae*: X (Oct–Dec)
____ Great Southern White *Ascia monuste*: C (Jan–Dec)
____ **Giant White** *Ganyra josephina*: O (Mar–Jan)
____ Falcate Orangetip *Anthocharis midea*: O (Feb–Apr)

Sulphurs—Subfamily Coliadinae

____ Orange Sulphur *Colias eurytheme*: U (Jan–Dec)
____ Southern Dogface *Colias cesonia* [*Zerene c.*]: C (Jan–Dec)
____ **White Angled-Sulphur** *Anteos clorinde*: O (Mar–May, Jul–Jan)
____ **Yellow Angled-Sulphur** *Anteos maerula*: O (Feb–Dec)
____ Cloudless Sulphur *Phoebis sennae*: A (Jan–Dec)
____ Orange-barred Sulphur *Phoebis philea*: U, L (Apr, Jul–Jan)
____ Large Orange Sulphur *Phoebis agarithe*: C (Jan–Dec)
____ **Tailed Sulphur** *Phoebis neocypris*: X (Oct, Nov)
____ **Statira Sulphur** *Phoebis statira* [*Aphrissa s.*]: X (Feb, Jun)
____ Lyside Sulphur *Kricogonia lyside*: A (Jan–Dec)
____ Barred Yellow *Eurema daira*: X (Aug–Nov)
____ **Ghost Yellow** *Eurema albula*: X (Nov)
____ Boisduval's Yellow *Eurema boisduvaliana*: U, L (Apr–Jan)
____ Mexican Yellow *Eurema mexicana*: R (Jan–Dec)
____ **Salome Yellow** *Eurema salome*: H (Sep)
____ Tailed Orange *Eurema proterpia* [*Pyrisitia p.*]: U (Jun–Jan)
____ Little Yellow *Eurema lisa* [*Pyrisitia l.*]: C (Jan–Dec)
____ **Mimosa Yellow** *Eurema nise* [*Pyrisitia n.*]: U, L (Aug–Jan)
____ Dina Yellow *Eurema dina* [*Pyrisitia d.*]: X (Apr, Jul, Sep)
____ Sleepy Orange *Eurema nicippe* [*Abaeis n.*]: A (Jan–Dec)
____ Dainty Sulphur *Nathalis iole*: C (Jan–Dec)

Mimic-Whites—Subfamily Dismorphiinae

___ **Costa-spotted Mimic-White** *Enantia albania*: H (Sep)

Gossamer-wing Butterflies—Family Lycaenidae

Hairstreaks—Subfamily Theclinae

___ **Strophius Hairstreak** *Allosmaitia strophius*: H (Oct, Nov)
___ Great Purple Hairstreak *Atlides halesus*: U (Jan–Dec)
___ **Gold-bordered Hairstreak** *Rekoa palegon*: H (Nov)
___ **Marius Hairstreak** *Rekoa marius*: X (Sep–Dec)
___ **Black Hairstreak** *Ocaria ocrisia*: X (Jan, Nov)
___ Telea Hairstreak *Chlorostrymon telea*: H (Jun)
___ **Silver-banded Hairstreak** *Chlorostrymon simaethis*: U, L (Jan–Dec)
___ Oak Hairstreak *Satyrium favonius*: X (Apr, May)
___ **Clench's Greenstreak** *Cyanophrys miserabilis*: R, L (Apr–Dec)
___ **Goodson's Greenstreak** *Cyanophrys goodsoni*: X (May–Dec)
___ **Tropical Greenstreak** *Cyanophrys herodotus*: X (May, Jun, Oct)
___ **Xami Hairstreak** *Callophrys xami*: C, L (Jan–Dec)
___ **Aquamarine Hairstreak** *Oenomaus ortygnus*: X (Nov, Dec)
___ Gray Hairstreak *Strymon melinus*: C (Jan–Dec)
___ **Red-crescent Scrub-Hairstreak** *Strymon rufofusca*: O (Mar–Jan)
___ Red-lined Scrub-Hairstreak *Strymon bebrycia*: O (Oct–Nov)
___ **Yojoa Scrub-Hairstreak** *Strymon yojoa*: O (Apr, Oct–Jan)
___ **White Scrub-Hairstreak** *Strymon albata*: R (Apr, Jun–Dec)
___ Lacey's Scrub-Hairstreak *Strymon alea*: U, L (Apr, Oct–Dec)
___ Mallow Scrub-Hairstreak *Strymon istapa*: C (Jan–Dec)
___ **Tailless Scrub-Hairstreak** *Strymon cestri*: X (Mar)
___ **Lantana Scrub-Hairstreak** *Strymon bazochii*: O (Jan–Mar, May, Oct–Dec)
___ **Ruddy Hairstreak** *Electrostrymon sangala*: X (Apr, Oct–Dec)
___ **Muted Hairstreak** *Electrostrymon canus* [*E. joya*]: X (?)

___ Dusky-blue Groundstreak *Calycopis isobeon*: C (Jan–Dec)
___ Mountain Groundstreak *Ziegleria guzanta* X (Jan)
___ **Red-spotted Hairstreak** *Tmolus echion*: H (May)
___ **Pearly-gray Hairstreak** *Siderus tephraeus* [*Strephonota t.*]: X (Sep–Dec)
___ **Clytie Ministreak** *Ministrymon clytie*: C, L (Jan–Dec)
___ **Gray Ministreak** *Ministrymon azia*: O (Mar–Oct)

Blues—Subfamily Polyommatinae

___ Western Pygmy-Blue *Brephidium exile*: C, L (Jan–Dec)
___ Cassius Blue *Leptotes cassius*: O (Jan–Dec)
___ Marine Blue *Leptotes marina*: U (Jan–Dec)
___ Cyna Blue *Zizula cyna*: R (Mar–Jan)
___ Ceraunus Blue *Hemiargus ceraunus*: C (Jan–Dec)
___ Reakirt's Blue *Hemiargus isola* [*Echinargus i.*]: C (Jan–Dec)
___ Eastern Tailed-Blue *Everes comyntas* [*Cupido c.*]: R, L (Jul, Aug)

Metalmarks—Family Riodinidae

___ Fatal Metalmark *Calephelis nemesis*: C (Jan–Dec)
___ Rounded Metalmark *Calephelis perditalis*: C (Jan–Dec)
___ Rawson's Metalmark *Calephelis rawsoni*: R, L (Feb–Nov)
___ **Red-bordered Metalmark** *Caria ino*: C (Jan–Dec)
___ **Blue Metalmark** *Lasaia sula*: U, L (Jan–Dec)
___ **Red-bordered Pixie** *Melanis pixe*: U, L (Apr, May, Jul–Jan)
___ **Curve-winged Metalmark** *Emesis emesia*: R (Feb, May–Dec)
___ **Falcate Metalmark** *Emesis tenedia*: H (Oct)
___ **Narrow-winged Metalmark** *Apodemia multiplaga*: X (Oct, Nov)
___ **Walker's Metalmark** *Apodemia walkeri*: R (May–Aug, Oct–Dec)

Brush-footed Butterflies—Family Nymphalidae

Snouts—Subfamily Libytheinae

___ American Snout *Libytheana carinenta*: A (Jan–Dec)

Heliconians and Fritillaries—Subfamily Heliconiinae

___ Gulf Fritillary *Agraulis vanillae*: C (Jan–Dec)
___ **Mexican Silverspot** *Dione moneta*: O (Apr–Jan)
___ **Banded Orange Heliconian** *Dryadula phaetusa*: X (Mar, Aug, Nov)
___ **Julia Heliconian** *Dryas iulia*: U, L (Jan–Dec)
___ **Isabella's Heliconian** *Eueides isabella*: R (Apr, May, Jul, Oct–Dec)
___ **Zebra Heliconian** *Heliconius charithonia*: U, L (Jan–Dec)
___ **Erato Heliconian** *Heliconius erato*: R (Jan, Jun, Aug, Dec)
___ Variegated Fritillary *Euptoieta claudia*: C (Jan–Dec)
___ **Mexican Fritillary** *Euptoieta hegesia*: U, L (Mar, Jul–Dec)

True Brushfoots—Subfamily Nymphalinae

___ Theona Checkerspot *Thessalia theona* [*Chlosyne t.*]: U (Mar–Jan)
___ Bordered Patch *Chlosyne lacinia*: C (Jan–Dec)
___ Definite Patch *Chlosyne definita*: C, L (Jul–Jan)
___ **Banded Patch** *Chlosyne endeis*: X (Mar, Oct–Dec)
___ Crimson Patch *Chlosyne janais*: O (Jul, Oct–Dec)
___ **Rosita Patch** *Chlosyne rosita*: H (Oct)
___ **Red-spotted Patch** *Chlosyne marina* [*C. melitaeoides*]: H (Oct)
___ **Elf** *Microtia elva*: X (Aug)
___ Tiny Checkerspot *Dymasia dymas*: R, L (Oct, Nov)
___ Elada Checkerspot *Texola elada*: C, L (Feb–Dec)
___ Texan Crescent *Phyciodes texana* [*Anathanassa t.*]: C, L (Jan–Dec)
___ **Pale-banded Crescent** *Phyciodes tulcis* [*Anathanassa t.*]: R, L (Mar, May, Oct–Dec)
___ **Black Crescent** *Phyciodes ptolyca* [*Anathanassa p.*]: X (Mar, Dec)

___ **Chestnut Crescent** *Phyciodes argentea [Anathanassa a.]*: X (Nov, Dec)

___ Vesta Crescent *Phyciodes vesta [P. graphica]*: C (Jan–Dec)

___ Phaon Crescent *Phyciodes phaon*: C (Jan–Dec)

___ Pearl Crescent *Phyciodes tharos*: C (Jan–Dec)

Anglewings, Ladies, and Buckeyes— Subfamily Nymphalinae

___ Question Mark *Polygonia interrogationis*: U (Jan–Dec)

___ Mourning Cloak *Nymphalis antiopa:* X (Apr)

___ American Lady *Vanessa virginiensis*: C (Jan–Dec)

___ Painted Lady *Vanessa cardui*: C (Jan–Dec)

___ West Coast Lady *Vanessa annabella*: X (Apr, Nov)

___ Red Admiral *Vanessa atalanta*: C (Jan–Dec)

___ Mimic *Hypolimnas misippus*: X (Aug)

___ Common Buckeye *Junonia coenia*: C (Jan–Dec)

___ Tropical Buckeye *Junonia evarete*: R (Jan–Dec)

___ Mangrove Buckeye *Junonia genoveva*: R, L (Mar, Apr, Oct, Nov)

___ **White Peacock** *Anartia jatrophae*: C (Jan–Dec)

___ **Banded Peacock** *Anartia fatima*: R (Mar–Jan)

___ **Malachite** *Siproeta stelenes*: O (Jan–Dec)

___ **Rusty-tipped Page** *Siproeta epaphus*: X (Nov)

Admirals and Relatives—Subfamily Limenitidinae

___ Red-spotted Purple *Limenitis arthemis*: X (Nov)

___ Viceroy *Limenitis archippus*: R, L (Apr–Nov)

___ **Band-celled Sister** *Adelpha fessonia*: R (Jan–Apr, Jul–Dec)

___ California Sister *Adelpha bredowii*: X (Nov)

___ **Spot-celled Sister** *Adelpha basiloides*: X (Nov)

___ **Common Banner** *Epiphile adrasta*: R (Oct–Jan)

___ **Mexican Bluewing** *Myscelia ethusa*: U, L (Jan–Dec)

___ Blackened Bluewing *Myscelia cyananthe*: H (Oct)

___ **Dingy Purplewing** *Eunica monima*: O (Jun–Nov)

___ Florida Purplewing *Eunica tatila*: X (Aug–Oct)

___ **Blue-eyed Sailor** *Dynamine dyonis*: R, L (Jun, Sep–Dec)

___ Common Mestra *Mestra amymone*: C (Jan–Dec)

___ **Red Rim** *Biblis hyperia*: O, L (Mar, May, Jul–Jan)

___ **Red Cracker** *Hamadryas amphinome*: X (Jan, Sep)

___ **Gray Cracker** *Hamadryas februa*: O (Jul–Dec)

___ **Variable Cracker** *Hamadryas feronia*: X (Oct–Dec)

___ **Guatemalan Cracker** *Hamadryas guatemalena*: X (Aug, Oct–Feb)

___ Orion Cecropian *Historis odius*: H (Jul)

___ **Blomfild's Beauty** *Smyrna blomfildia*: X (Nov–Jan)

___ **Waiter Daggerwing** *Marpesia coresia* [*M. zerynthia*]: X (Jul)

___ **Many-banded Daggerwing** *Marpesia chiron*: O (Feb, Apr, Jul–Oct)

___ **Ruddy Daggerwing** *Marpesia petreus*: O (Feb, Apr, Jul–Nov)

Leafwings—Subfamily Charaxinae

___ Tropical Leafwing *Anaea aidea*: C, L (Jan–Dec)

___ Goatweed Leafwing *Anaea andria*: U, L (Mar–Dec)

___ Angled Leafwing *Anaea glycerium* [*Memphis g.*]: X (Jul, Aug)

___ **Pale-spotted Leafwing** *Anaea pithyusa* [*Memphis p.*]: R (Mar, Jul–Jan)

Emperors—Subfamily Apaturinae

___ Hackberry Emperor *Asterocampa celtis*: C, L (Mar–Dec)

___ Empress Leilia *Asterocampa leilia*: C, L (Feb–Dec)

___ Tawny Emperor *Asterocampa clyton*: C, L (Apr–Feb)

___ **Pavon Emperor** *Doxocopa pavon*: R (May, Aug–Dec)

___ **Silver Emperor** *Doxocopa laure*: R (Jul–Dec)

Satyrs—Subfamily Satyrinae

___ Gemmed Satyr *Cyllopsis gemma*: C, L (Jan–Dec)

___ Carolina Satyr *Hermeuptychia sosybius*: A, L (Jan–Dec)

Clearwings—Subfamily Ithomiinae

____ **Klug's Clearwing** *Dircenna klugii*: H (Apr)

Monarchs—Subfamily Danainae

____ Monarch *Danaus plexippus*: C (Jan–Dec)
____ Queen *Danaus gilippus*: A (Jan–Dec)
____ **Soldier** *Danaus eresimus*: U (Apr–Jan)

Skippers—Family Hesperiidae

Spread-wing Skippers—Subfamily Pyrginae

____ **Beautiful Beamer** *Phocides belus*: X (Apr)
____ **Guava Skipper** *Phocides polybius*: U (Jan–Dec)
____ **Mercurial Skipper** *Proteides mercurius*: R (Apr, Oct)
____ **Broken Silverdrop** *Epargyreus exadeus*: X (Oct)
____ Hammock Skipper *Polygonus leo*: X (Mar, Apr, Sep–Nov)
____ Manuel's Skipper *Polygonus manueli* [*P. savigno*]: H (Aug–Oct)
____ White-striped Longtail *Chioides catillus* [*C. albofasciatus*]: U (Jan–Dec)
____ **Zilpa Longtail** *Chioides zilpa*: O (Mar–Apr, Sep–Nov)
____ **Gold-spotted Aguna** *Aguna asander*: R (Apr–Jan)
____ **Emerald Aguna** *Aguna claxon*: R (Jan, Oct, Nov)
____ **Tailed Aguna** *Aguna metophis*: O (Aug–Jan)
____ **Mottled Longtail** *Typhedanus undulatus*: H (Aug–Nov)
____ **Mexican Longtail** *Polythrix mexicanus*: X (Jul, Oct)
____ **Eight-spotted Longtail** *Polythrix octomaculata*: X (Mar, Sep, Oct)
____ **White-crescent Longtail** *Codatractus alcaeus*: X (Oct)
____ Long-tailed Skipper *Urbanus proteus*: U (Jan–Dec)
____ **Pronus Longtail** *Urbanus pronus*: X (Oct)
____ **Double-striped Longtail** *Urbanus belli*: H (Jun)
____ **Esmeralda Longtail** *Urbanus esmeraldus*: X (Aug)
____ Dorantes Longtail *Urbanus dorantes*: U (Jan–Dec)

___ **Teleus Longtail** *Urbanus teleus*: R (May–Jan)

___ **Tanna Longtail** *Urbanus tanna*: X (Jun, Dec)

___ **Plain Longtail** *Urbanus simplicius*: X (Apr)

___ **Brown Longtail** *Urbanus procne*: C (Jan–Dec)

___ **White-tailed Longtail** *Urbanus doryssus*: X (Mar–Jul, Oct, Nov)

___ **Two-barred Flasher** *Astraptes fulgerator*: O (Mar–Jan)

___ **Small-spotted Flasher** *Astraptes egregius*: X (Oct)

___ **Frosted Flasher** *Astraptes alardus*: X (Jun, Sep, Oct)

___ **Gilbert's Flasher** *Astraptes gilberti* [*A. alector*]: X (Mar, Oct)

___ **Yellow-tipped Flasher** *Astraptes anaphus*: R (Apr, Sep–Nov)

___ Coyote Cloudywing *Achalarus toxeus*: U (Jan–Dec)

___ **Jalapus Cloudywing** *Achalarus jalapus* [*Thessia j.*]: X (Jul–Nov)

___ Northern Cloudywing *Thorybes pylades*: X (?)

___ **Potrillo Skipper** *Cabares potrillo*: U (Apr–Feb)

___ **Fritzgaertner's Flat** *Celaenorrhinus fritzgaertneri*: X (Feb, Jul, Sep, Nov)

___ **Stallings' Flat** *Celaenorrhinus stallingsi*: R (Jun, Aug, Oct–Dec)

___ **Falcate Skipper** *Spathilepia clonius*: R (May–Jul, Oct–Dec)

___ **Mimosa Skipper** *Cogia calchas*: C (Jan–Dec)

___ Acacia Skipper *Cogia hippalus*: X (Apr, Aug, Sep)

___ Outis Skipper *Cogia outis*: X (Apr)

___ **Starred Skipper** *Arteurotia tractipennis*: X (Sep, Nov)

___ **Purplish-black Skipper** *Nisoniades rubescens*: X (Oct, Nov)

___ **Glazed Pellicia** *Pellicia arina*: O (Apr, Jun–Jan)

___ **Morning Glory Pellicia** *Pellicia dimidiata*: X (Oct)

___ **Red-studded Skipper** *Noctuana stator*: X (Oct)

___ **Mottled Bolla** *Bolla clytius*: X (Jun–Nov)

___ **Obscure Bolla** *Bolla brennus*: H (Oct)

___ Golden-headed Scallopwing *Staphylus ceos*: R (Mar–Dec)

___ **Mazans Scallopwing** *Staphylus mazans*: C (Jan–Dec)

___ **Variegated Skipper** *Gorgythion begga*: X (Mar, Dec)

___ **Blue-studded Skipper** *Sostrata bifasciata* [*S. nordica*]: X (Oct)

___ **Tropical Duskywing** *Anastrus sempiternus*: X (Oct, Nov)

___ **Hoary Skipper** *Carrhenes canescens*: O (Feb–Jun, Oct–Dec)

___ **Glassy-winged Skipper** *Xenophanes tryxus*: X (Jul–Nov)

___ Texas Powdered-Skipper *Systasea pulverulenta*: U (Jan–Dec)

___ Sickle-winged Skipper *Achlyodes thraso* [*Eantis tamenund*]: A (Jan–Dec)

___ **Pale Sicklewing** *Achlyodes pallida*: X (Oct–Dec)

___ **Hermit Skipper** *Grais stigmatica*: O (Apr, May, Jul–Nov)

___ **Brown-banded Skipper** *Timochares ruptifasciatus*: O (Feb–Jun, Aug–Dec)

___ **White-patched Skipper** *Chiomara asychis* [*C. georgina*]: C (Jan–Dec)

___ False Duskywing *Gesta gesta* [*G. invisus*]: O (Mar, Apr, Aug)

___ Horace's Duskywing *Erynnis horatius*: R (Apr, Oct, Nov)

___ Mournful Duskywing *Erynnis tristis*: U (Jan–Dec)

___ Funereal Duskywing *Erynnis funeralis*: U (Jan–Dec)

___ Common Checkered-Skipper *Pyrgus communis*: R (Jan–Dec)

___ White Checkered-Skipper *Pyrgus albescens*: C (Jan–Dec)

___ Tropical Checkered-Skipper *Pyrgus oileus*: C (Jan–Dec)

___ Desert Checkered-Skipper *Pyrgus philetas*: U (Mar–Nov)

___ Erichson's White-Skipper *Heliopetes domicella* [*Heliopyrgus d.*]: R (Sep–Dec)

___ Laviana White-Skipper *Heliopetes laviana*: C (Jan–Dec)

___ Turk's-cap White-Skipper *Heliopetes macaira*: U (Jan–Dec)

___ **Veined White-Skipper** *Heliopetes arsalte*: X (Oct)

___ Common Streaky-Skipper *Celotes nessus*: R (Jan, Mar–Oct)

___ Common Sootywing *Pholisora catullus*: U (Mar–Nov)

___ Saltbush Sootywing *Hesperopsis alpheus*: R, L (Apr–Nov)

Skipperlings—Subfamily Heteropterinae

___ **Small-spotted Skipperling** *Piruna microstictus* [*P. penaea*]: X (Oct)

Grass-Skippers—Subfamily Hesperiinae

___ **Malicious Skipper** *Synapte malitiosa* [*S. pecta*]: R (Apr–Dec)

___ **Salenus Skipper** *Synapte salenus*: X (Aug–Oct)

___ **Redundant Skipper** *Corticea corticea*: H (Sep–Dec)

___ **Pale-rayed Skipper** *Vidius perigenes*: O, L (Mar–Nov)

___ **Violet-patched Skipper** *Monca tyrtaeus* [*M. crispinus*]: O (Mar, May–Jun, Oct–Dec)

___ Julia's Skipper *Nastra julia*: C (Jan–Dec)

___ Swarthy Skipper *Nastra lherminier*: X (Nov)

___ **Fawn-spotted Skipper** *Cymaenes odilia* [*C. trebius*]: U (Jan–Dec)

___ Clouded Skipper *Lerema accius*: C (Jan–Dec)

___ **Liris Skipper** *Lerema liris*: X (Jul–Oct)

___ **Fantastic Skipper** *Vettius fantasos*: X (Oct–Dec)

___ **Green-backed Ruby-eye** *Perichares philetes*: X (Nov, Dec)

___ **Osca Skipper** *Rhinthon osca*: X (Oct)

___ **Double-dotted Skipper** *Decinea percosius*: O, L (Mar–Dec)

___ **Hidden-ray Skipper** *Conga chydaea*: X (Jul–Oct)

___ Least Skipper *Ancyloxypha numitor*: R, L (Mar–Nov)

___ Tropical Least Skipper *Ancyloxypha arene*: R, L (Jul)

___ Orange Skipperling *Copaeodes aurantiaca*: U (Jan–Dec)

___ Southern Skipperling *Copaeodes minima*: C (Jan–Dec)

___ Fiery Skipper *Hylephila phyleus*: C (Jan–Dec)

___ Whirlabout *Polites vibex*: C (Jan–Dec)

___ Southern Broken-Dash *Wallengrenia otho*: C (Jan–Dec)

___ Delaware Skipper *Anatrytone logan*: X (Jun)

___ Sachem *Atalopedes campestris*: C (Jan–Dec)

___ **Common Mellana** *Quasimellana eulogius*: O (Apr–Feb)

___ Dun Skipper *Euphyes vestris*: O (Mar–Dec)

___ Nysa Roadside-Skipper *Amblyscirtes nysa*: U (Feb–Oct)

___ Celia's Roadside-Skipper *Amblyscirtes celia*: C (Jan–Dec)

___ Dotted Roadside-Skipper *Amblyscirtes eos*: X (?)

___ Eufala Skipper *Lerodea eufala*: C (Jan–Dec)

___ **Olive-clouded Skipper** *Lerodea dysaules* [*L. arabus*]: U (Jan–Dec)

___ Brazilian Skipper *Calpodes ethlius*: U, L (Jan–Dec)
___ Obscure Skipper *Panoquina panoquinoides*: U, L (Jan–Dec)
___ Ocola Skipper *Panoquina ocola*: C (Jan–Dec)
___ **Hecebolus Skipper** *Panoquina hecebola*: R (Jul–Dec)
___ **Purple-washed Skipper** *Panoquina sylvicola* [*P. lucas*]: O (Aug–Jan)
___ **Evans' Skipper** *Panoquina fusina* [*P. evansi*]: X (Oct, Nov)
___ **Violet-banded Skipper** *Nyctelius nyctelius*: O (May, Sep–Feb)

Giant-Skippers—Subfamily Megathyminae

___ Yucca Giant-Skipper *Megathymus yuccae*: O, L (Feb–Apr)
___ Manfreda Giant-Skipper *Stallingsia maculosa* [*S. maculosus*]: H (May, Sep–Nov)

Hypothetical Species

Common (Mylotes) Cattleheart *Parides eurimedes*
Eastern Tiger Swallowtail *Papilio glaucus*
Palamedes Swallowtail *Papilio palamedes*
Victorine Swallowtail *Papilio victorinus*
Mexican Dartwhite *Catasticta nimbice*
Mexican Cycadian *Eumaeus toxea*
Apricot Sulphur *Phoebis argante*
Harvester *Feniseca tarquinius*
Creamy Stripe-Streak *Arawacus jada*
Eastern Pygmy-Blue *Brephidium isophthalma*
Green Longwing *Philaethria dido*
Ardys Crescent *Anthanassa ardys*
Huastecan Crescent *Tegosa anieta*
Orange Mapwing *Hypanartia lethe*
Common Morpho *Morpho peleides*
Tiger Mimic-Queen *Lycorea cleobaea*
Rainbow Skipper *Phocides urania*

Silver-spotted Skipper *Epargyreus clarus*
Euribates Skipper *Dyscophellus euribates*
Skinner's Cloudywing *Achalarus albociliatus*
Hayhurst's Scallopwing *Staphylus hayhurstii*
Foldless Checkered-Skipper *Pyrgus adepta*
Mexican Sootywing *Pholisora mejicana*
Ubiquitous Skipper *Callimormus saturnus*
Glowing Skipper *Anatrytone mazai*
Chestnut-marked Skipper *Thespieus macareus*

Index of Plant Names

The common and scientific names of plant species mentioned in the "When and Where" narratives and elsewhere in the text are indexed here to assist in researching them further. They are primarily the larval food-plants of butterflies. The plant names are those used in the *Checklist of the Vascular Plants of Texas* by Stephen L. Hatch and associates (1990).

Index of Scientific Names of Butterflies

Scientific names used in this book are those established by the North American Butterfly Association. When scientific names published by Opler and Warren (2002) differ, those names are included with a reference to the NABA scientific name..

Index of Common Names of Butterflies

Common names used in this book are those established by the North American Butterfly Association. Alternate names and historical names mentioned in the text are included with a reference to the current NABA common name. Page numbers in **boldface** indicate main species accounts..

Butterflies of the
Lower Rio Grande Valley